W9-CDO-976

THE LOYALIST EXPERIENCE IN NORTH CAROLINA

for
G. A. F.

THE LOYALIST EXPERIENCE IN NORTH CAROLINA

by

Carole Watterson Troxler

Raleigh 1976

Copyright, 1976, by the North Carolina Department
of Cultural Resources, Division of Archives and History

N.C.
975.603
T

c. 3

ACKNOWLEDGMENTS

Mrs. Geneva Caulfield graciously loaned me microfilm made by her late husband, Thomas E. Caulfield. References to the Legislative Papers and the Board of War Papers, Military Collection, in the North Carolina State Archives are from his film. Elon College provided a grant for the typing of the manuscript, which Mrs. Betty Parker performed ably and cooperatively and which Mrs. Emma Lewis skillfully proofread. I am grateful to George Troxler for reading the manuscript. I appreciate deeply George Stevenson's suggestions, Jerry Cashion's reading of much of the manuscript, and Gayle Fishel's untiring labors.

TABLE OF CONTENTS

INTRODUCTION vii

I. LOYALIST RESPONSES TO THE REVOLUTION TO 1780 1

Disapproval, resistance, and avoidance 2

Conspiracy: the gourd patch tories 12

Accommodation and defiance 17

II. WAR AND LITIGATION 21

Military service 21

The loss of property 29

Loss by debt: the trials of Mary Dowd 32

Some other litigants 35

III. THE EXILES 37

In London 40

In East Florida 41

In the Bahama Islands 44

In Nova Scotia and New Brunswick 45

Black loyalists and Sierra Leone 49

In Upper Canada 54

IV. CONCLUSION 56

NOTES 59

NOTE ON SOURCES 66

Burlesque on the Loyalists

INTRODUCTION: THE LOYALISTS AND THE HISTORIANS

It is a commonplace remark nowadays that the loyalists lost both the Revolutionary War and its history. In the confident youth of the new republic, the earliest American historians despised the loyalists, or "tories." They gave the loyalists no serious attention, for it was assumed that they had not been a part of the American Revolution and the making of the nation. Loyalists retained a popular image as traitors and misfits, good only for tarring and feathering. As late as 1844, James Knox Polk in his presidential campaign learned that his grandfather's association with the British during their occupation of Charlotte was a mighty smear in the hands of his opponents.[1]

Curiosity about loyalists has emerged at times when complexities of the national experience have been inescapable and have rendered a simplistic view of the nation's origins inadequate.[2] Thus the period of the Civil War produced the pioneering effort in loyalist studies, Lorenzo Sabine's *Biographical Sketches of the Loyalists of the American Revolution* (Boston: 1864. Reprinted by Kennikat Press, 1966). Sabine's work demonstrated that the Revolution was a civil war, a point frequently made during the Revolution but generally ignored after its conclusion. Moses Coit Tyler's study of loyalist writers *(American Historical Review,* I [1895], 24-94) came at a time when Americans were questioning the nature of their nation amid a conflict between rural and urban values. Soon it was followed by a survey of the problems that loyalists presented to the state governments and to the British ministry: Claude H. Van Tyne, *The Loyalists in the American Revolution* (New York: Macmillan, 1902. Reprinted by Peter Smith, 1959).

After this beginning, statewide studies of loyalists appeared during the 1920s and 1930s as published monographs and dissertations of varying quality. Robert O. DeMond, *The Loyalists in North Carolina during the Revolution* (Durham:1940. Reprinted by Archon Books, 1964), pointed out the diversity and complexity of North Carolina loyalists and the importance of local issues there.

As the reprint dates of the works cited above begin to indicate, American interest in the loyalists surged in the 1960s and 1970s. The bicentennial of the American Revolution has heightened the interest, for one result of the research of the past two decades has been the conviction that the American Revolutionary experience cannot be understood apart from the loyalists.[3]

Who were the loyalists? Groups of people whom a casual inquirer might expect to have identified their well-being with British rule included: British merchants, officeholders under crown authority, Anglican clergymen, recent immigrants. Most of the loyalists were not so obvious. On present knowledge their cultural, economic, occupational, racial, ethnic, class, religious, and age backgrounds were virtually indistinguishable from those of other Americans who took the revolutionary course.

The complexity is less puzzling when viewed at close range. William Nelson has suggested that loyalists tended to be members of minority groups and revolutionaries tended to be members of dominant groups *within their immediate environment.* Thus, for example, most Anglicans might be loyalists in New England, where theirs was not the established church, while southern Anglicans were leading revolutionaries. Nelson observed,

> Taking all the groups and factions, sects, classes, and inhabitants of regions that seem to have been Tory, they have but one thing in common: they represented conscious minorities, people who felt weak and threatened.... Almost all the Loyalists were, in one way or another, more afraid of America than they were Britain.... Being fairly certain that they would be in a permanent minority (as Quakers or oligarchs or frontiersmen or Dutchmen [for example]) they could not find much comfort in a theory of government that assured them of sovereign equality with other Americans *as individuals*.... Most of them shared [a] suspicion of a political order based on the "common good" if the common good was to be defined by a numerical majority.[4]

While this does not explain all loyalism, it has been borne out by much of the recent scholarship.

How did the loyalists' perception of the Revolution and the British Empire differ from that of the revolutionaries? Here insight is provided by Robert Calhoon's analysis of loyalists' writings. He observed that they often expressed the belief that each colony had acknowledged English law from the time of its founding and that Britain had exercised continuous authority over it. This view stood in opposition to the revolutionary doctrine that the colonies had originated in a state of nature and had made a compact with Britain. Theology was a basic ground of division between revolutionary and loyalist perceptions. This conflict generally was along Calvinist versus rationalist lines, with the loyalists or proto-loyalists holding to a rationalist interpretation. They advocated American resistance to British policies, and some of them led it, but for them the purpose of resistance was to communicate with the men in the British government and to appeal to their reason.[5] Many of them believed that the ideal solution to governmental crisis was some kind of an American Parliament to represent, tax, and legislate for the colonies alone. Self-styled moderates, they refused to go along with ideas and actions which they thought were too radical.[6]

The majority of the loyalists left no written expressions of their attitudes. What was their motivation? The challenge of the inarticulate loyalists perhaps will be answered in the future by the retrieval and analysis of data about them from incidental and non-narrative sources, such as tax assessments, jury lists, land records, and merchants' accounts. Materials for the study of loyalists are being made more accessible by the Program for Loyalist Studies and Publications. A joint effort of American, British and Canadian scholars, its work is a fruitful celebration of two bicentennials: of the American Revolution in 1976 and of the founding of New Brunswick in 1984.[7]

Early revolutionaries expressed their own "loyalty" in this motif which adorned the Minute Book of the Surry County Committee of Safety. Secretary of State's Papers, N.C.A.

I. LOYALIST RESPONSES TO THE REVOLUTION TO 1780

When the group that would spearhead the Revolution in the frontier county of Rowan met for the first time in August, 1774, their opening salvo was this unanimous resolution:

> That we will at all times, when ever we are called upon for that Purpose, maintain and defend at the Expense of our Lives and our fortunes, his Majesty's Right and Title to the Crown of Great Britain, and his Dominions in America, to whose royal person and government, we profess all due Obedience & Fidelity.[8]

Such resolutions were common among the committees of safety. They were, of course, making the point that their quarrel was with Parliament over taxation and not with the king over sovereignty. Today, declarations of loyalty made by men who would lead America to independence are reminders that the goals of the revolutionaries shifted with the torrent of events. Their changes were watched by unsympathetic contemporaries like Collin Shaw of Cumberland County, in 1778 an exile in New York. Refusing to pin his hopes for peace on the Carlisle Peace Commission's chances of success, Shaw observed that "the king['s] proposels Lastly to America ... is ye verey thing the people in Carolina wanted as they use to tell me ... now I have Reason to be sure that they will Except of the verey things they were wanting as it is now in there offer. ..."[9] Shaw's pessimism may indicate that he understood the nature of revolution better than he was willing to admit.

Since the positions of revolutionaries changed with time and events, it is not surprising that the opponents and victims of the Revolution experienced similar shifts. Here are three examples of opposition to the revolutionary course of events, drawn respectively from the beginning, the middle, and the end of the war: 1) objection to the activities of the Continental Congress or the provincial congress prior to the battles of Lexington and Concord; 2) refusal to absolve one's allegiance to the crown and to serve in the revolutionary militia when there were no British forces at hand; 3) fighting against one's revolutionary neighbors at the height of the civil war. Each of these actions could require distinct motivation and commitment. By choosing one, a person was at the time considered a loyalist, both by himself and by his neighbors, even though the word "loyalist" itself might not be used.

This is not to deny that there were men and women who consistently opposed the Revolution from start to finish—there were, and some of them appear in these pages—but it is to suggest that they were exceptional. The array of political opinion during the revolutionary years can be envisaged as one spectrum rather than two separate spectra of "revolutionaries" and "loyalists." During the long war, people moved from one shade to another, and some moved from one end to the other. That is why the attempt to identify "real" loyalists is an unrewarding exercise. Whether a person was a loyalist or a revolutionary often depends on what period during the Revolution is being investigated. Perhaps a look at the backgrounds against which people exhibited their loyalism can aid in understanding what happened in North Carolina during the American Revolution.

Disapproval, resistance, and avoidance

Long before any fighting began, opinions differed over the nonimportation movement. As in the other southern colonies, North Carolina merchants traded heavily with Britain. The local committees of safety reprimanded merchants who continued to do so against their orders and tried to prevent people from doing business with them. The attention marked these merchants as dissenters early in the conflict, a distinction that some of them retained and others did not.

The opinions of a merchant who refused to cooperate with the nonimportation movement were articulated by Andrew Miller of Halifax, whose trade was chiefly with Glasgow. In December, 1774, he refused the committee of safety's invitation to sign the nonimportation agreement, saying that he must first discharge his debts. The committee forbade trade with Miller. He commented that he did not lose a single customer as a result. Miller explained his stand as a refusal "to distress, my friends in Britain, merely because they could not Procure a Repeal of the Obnoxious Laws, tho they may exert their utmost Interest for that purpose."[10] Miller could not envision independence for the colonies in the near future, but he did expect a loosening of ties. In an analysis more pragmatic than conservative, he told a future governor of the state that

> in the Infant State of the Colonys, while they cannot subsist without the Protection of some Maritime Power such as Britain, It would be as well to Submit to the power of Legislation as exercised by them [Parliament] — except as to Taxation, and even that I

> would submit to for a while, untill we had got Manufactores amongst ourselves, of Cloth pow[d]er &c and our numbers a little increased, or our bounds more Circumscribed, our Slaves emancipated &&c[11]

In the months that followed, Miller disapproved of the Continental Congress as a challenge to legitimate authority. He detested the Declaratory Act, the Quebec Act, and the Boston Port Act, but he believed Parliament had a right to legislate for the colonies. Rather than impudently convene an illegal Congress, he believed the colonists should use their provincial assemblies to petition Parliament to withdraw the evil laws. He reprehended Virginia's call for troops as an irresponsible widening of the breach. Miller observed that Parliament taxed only luxuries and opined, "I rather think she [Britain] wishes to give up the power of Taxation, but will not be threatened out of it by a Congress or a Virginia Army."[12] To Andrew Miller, Britain's rule of the colonies seemed legitimate, firm, benevolent in intent, and necessary.[13]

People who were asked to sign a nonimportation agreement usually were required to make one or more additional promises. Although the promises varied in form, they stemmed from the Continental Association. After the North Carolina Convention adopted it in April, 1775, the committees of safety took it up as a badge of unity. They called in or hauled in persons whom they suspected of disapproving the committee's actions, interrogated them, and pressured them to sign a statement or take an oath.

Whether written or oral, the statement was referred to as the "test." The conditions ranged from a promise of neutrality to a promise to bear arms against British troops under the leadership of the provincial congress or the Continental Congress. Typically, the New Bern Committee of Safety considered a refusal to sign as a declaration "to the public, that they are enemies of the liberties of America." Accordingly the committee ordered the militia captains to take all arms and ammunition from refusers. Other actions intended to force compliance were posting of names as "enemies of America," threats, and imprisonment. The influencing of public opinion was an important concern of the committees of safety, and they had the power to make a man a "patriot" or a "tory."[14]

James Cotton's experience with such a "test" confirmed him in his loyalist tendencies. Cotton was a wealthy planter and officeholder in Anson County. A native of New England, he had been a justice of the peace and a member of the assembly. His offices as register of deeds, surveyor, and deputy collector help account for his unpopularity as a "placeman." When he refused to approve the local adaptation of the Continental Association in May, 1775, the Anson County Committee of Safety gave him two weeks to reconsider. When the period ended without Cotton's yielding, a group of armed men broke into his bedroom before he and his wife arose early one morning. They took him toward a place about twenty-five miles away, where the Cheraws and Anson committees of safety were to receive him. After travelling about five miles, Cotton treated his captors to rum. After ten more miles in the warm morning sun they stopped at a public house where he bought them cider and escaped.

Cotton returned home and hid in the woods for several days. Then he paid a visit to Governor Josiah Martin, who had fled from his palatial residence at New Bern to the security of a ship off the mouth of the Cape Fear River. In Cotton's absence, his revolution-prone neighbors laid waste to his crops, offered a reward for his capture, and warned that they would burn his house and mill and take his stock and slaves if he tried to return home. He did not remain long with the governor. Captured in Bladen County, Cotton was brought before the provincial congress at Hillsborough in August, 1775, along with two other Anson County men. Neither of the others was an official, but like Cotton they had refused to approve the Association. Cotton later said that the provincial congress gave the three of them the choice of changing their minds or being hanged that day. They signed the Association and went home. Six months later Cotton and his two companions stood together again — under the king's banner at Moore's Creek Bridge, North Carolina's first revolutionary battle.[15]

North Carolina revolutionaries eased into military action by sending troops to South Carolina and Virginia in November and December of 1775. By February, 1776, they had a fight on their hands at home.

During the autumn of 1775 the British government received glowing estimates of southern loyalism. The estimates came from the governors of the Carolinas and Virginia who were sheltering their dignity aboard British vessels, for their capitals were in the hands of revolutionaries. The governors pressed London with military schemes for their restoration. The most ambitious plans were those of North Carolina's Josiah Martin.

Martin laid before the secretary of state for the colonies a scheme for regaining the southern provinces. Central to his plan were Highland Scots who had settled in the Cape Fear Valley. There had been several waves of immigration, but the largest had occurred during the past decade. Martin declared that at least 3,000 Highlanders would be the nucleus of a loyal force that would swell to some 20,000 once British arms and support arrived. He predicted that with North Carolina secured, Virginia would be overawed. Communication with the loyalists in the back parts of South Carolina would bring provisions and recruits and facilitate a British restoration in Charles Town.[16]

The governor's optimism was rewarded. Early in January, 1776, he learned from the secretary that a southern campaign was in preparation. Five regiments with spare arms for 10,000 loyalists supposedly were on their way from Ireland to the Cape Fear River. There they were to be joined by an expedition commander and reinforcements from Boston and by Martin's North Carolina loyalists. With the cooperation of the Indian superintendent and the royal governors of Virginia and the Carolinas, a campaign would be planned for the restoration of governments loyal to Britain.[17]

The strategy was altered even before Martin received news of it. The Ireland sailing was repeatedly delayed, and it was learned that the Cape Fear River was not a safe place to land the army from Boston. Eventually the expedition's purpose of arming loyalists in order to restore British authority was abandoned. Instead, a new goal of establishing a loyalist asylum on Sullivan's Island at Charles Town resulted in a bungled attack there in June, 1776.[18]

On receiving his January dispatch, Martin authorized leaders in several interior counties to embody and arm men and called on all loyal subjects to join in the suppression of the rebellion. By February 15 all recruits were to be on the coast ready to join the expected British forces.

Martin thought that former regulators from the western counties would flock to join the Highlanders. He counted on their honoring their recent oaths to the crown and giving fresh vent to their distaste for tidewater politicians. The "Regulators" who marched east underwent several rounds of defeat and desertion, so that probably fewer than 100 were available when the fighting began. About 1,400 Highlanders assembled, more than one-half of them armed only with claymores, the broadsword characteristic of the region of their birth.

There was little fighting. The revolutionaries maneuvered the outnumbered loyalists into an awkward position among the swamps of the Black River and the Widow Moore's Creek. Trying to break out and launch a dawn attack, the loyalists scrambled onto the creek bridge. Their opponents had partially dismantled the bridge and greased the stringers, and the king's friends were sitting ducks.[19]

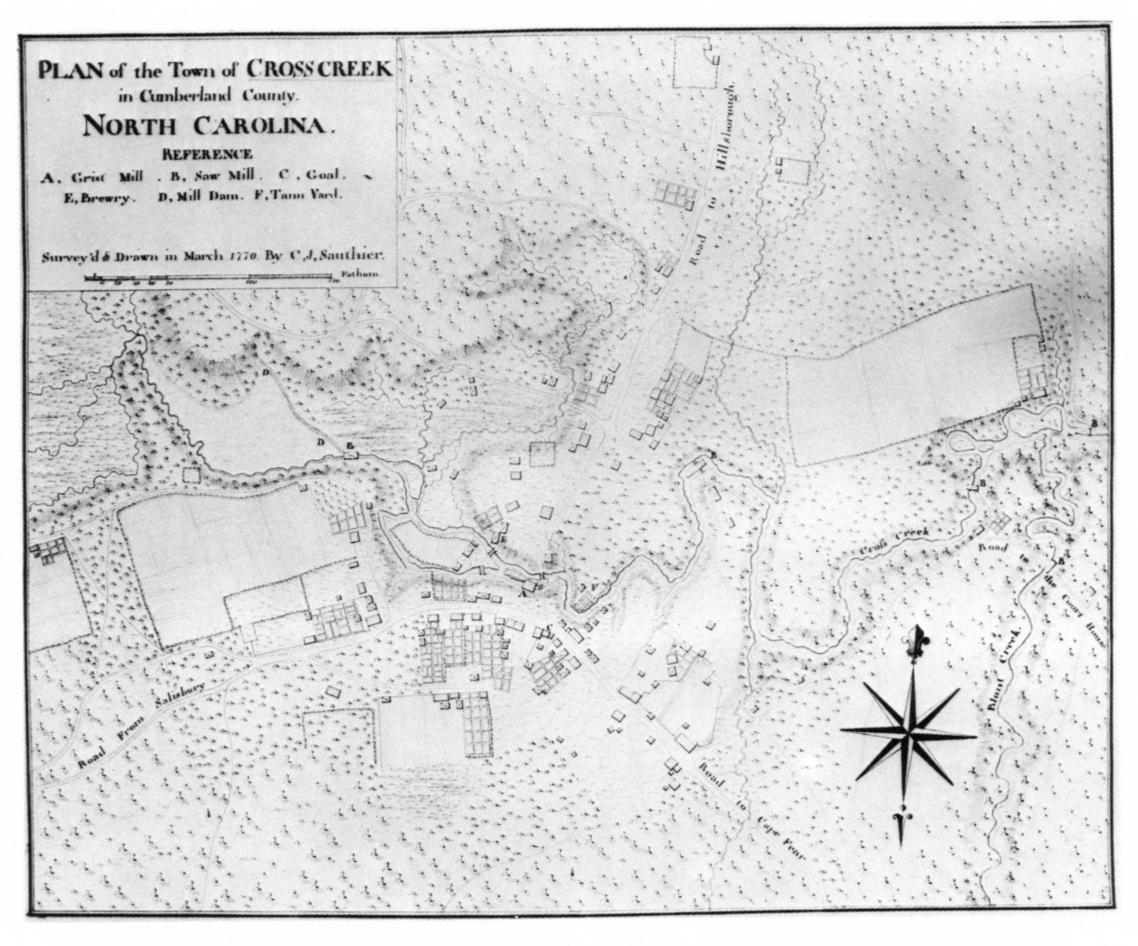

Before the Battle of Moore's Creek Bridge, the loyalists mustered at Cross Creek.

A revolutionary newspaper account exulted that the battle lasted only three minutes and that "this, we think, will effectively put a stop to Toryism in North Carolina."[20] It did put a stop to tory boldness. There was no loyalist effort of equal magnitude until the British occupation of South Carolina. With the defeat and Martin's departure a few months later, they had no central leadership and more significantly no assurance of British support against the revolutionaries. North Carolina loyalists were on their own in an increasingly hostile environment.

In the months following Moore's Creek Bridge the revolutionaries wanted to conciliate Highlanders who had not been leaders in the campaign. Captured privates were disarmed and allowed to return to their homes upon taking an oath not to take up arms against the revolutionary movement. The possibility of remaining at home depended on their neighbors' moods. Most of them tried to live inconspicuously and took no overt loyalist action until the British arrived in 1781, and some of them not even then, to General Charles Lord Cornwallis's chagrin.

Officers were another matter. About twenty officers and other prominent men were confined in North Carolina or released on bail. At least thirty men were imprisoned at Halifax and eventually at Philadelphia and Maryland, some for three years.

As with most other loyalist incarcerations early in the war, acceptance of the Revolution was the key that opened the jail door. Two years after Moore's Creek Bridge, Farquard Campbell's request for release was a matter-of-fact statement to his old associates, the North Carolina delegates to the Continental Congress, of his desire to return to the state and take its oath of allegiance. Campbell was neither humble nor bitter. He simply was "extremely desirous of Returning thither to live peaceably with my Family," and he did.[21] Michael Holt of Orange County was more apologetic. Soon after the battle he explained that when he responded to Martin's proclamation and commission he had not known what the "Tories" intended to do, and that he encouraged desertion after he learned. This, and a promise to take the oath, was enough to prompt the Orange County Committee of Safety to approve his release from Philadelphia.[22]

Officers who were not captured hid in the woods and swamps, as did some privates who had hostile neighbors. They received visits and food from their wives when they dared and moved about only at night. Some of them never lived at home again. After six months of such skulking, Joseph Mercer reached a British ship off Cape Fear and went to New York. Daniel Ray held out until he joined the British in South Carolina in 1780.[23]

The presence of the British in Pennsylvania and East Florida attracted men there after the Moore's Creek Bridge debacle. Eli Branson, a former regulator from Chatham County, reached the British forces in Pennsylvania about a year after the battle, after skulking in North Carolina and his native Virginia. He would return to Chatham County after the British left Philadelphia and continue an active loyalist. A recently settled Wilmington merchant, Alexander MacLean, later said that he conducted about seventy North Carolinians to General Sir William Howe's army. Such men commonly joined provincial, or loyalist, corps. One such unit that was to gain infamy in the South was Banastre Tarleton's British Legion. At least two officers from Moore's Creek Bridge joined it and thereby reduced their chances for resettlement in North Carolina. Other men went through the backcountry to the loyal colony of East Florida and from there joined the British forces in Georgia in 1779.[24]

From their confinement in Maryland some of the officers escaped and returned to North Carolina. One of them, Kenneth Stewart, said he had expected the British to welcome him home, and when he discovered that they were not there he took to the woods until 1780, when he joined the British forces at the Cheraws. Other returned officers went back to Pennsylvania with fresh North Carolina recruits.

Upon their release in 1779, most of the remaining officers returned south. The British foothold around Savannah was a great attraction. Some reached it, and some were captured along the way, both on land and sea. Thomas Wier is an extreme example of a Moore's Creek Bridge veteran who spent much of the war in confinement. After his release to New York late in 1778 he started toward Savannah but was captured at sea and imprisoned at Boston for six months. After a prisoner exchange, he headed for Savannah again. The French captured him at sea and sent him to Savannah only after their naval defeat there. Wier was in the Commissary General's Department at the start of Cornwallis's march through the Carolinas, but he was captured a fourth time just prior to the battle of Guilford Court House, and he spent the following five months a prisoner in Virginia. He rejoined Cornwallis at Portsmouth in time to fight at Yorktown.[25]

For loyalists who had marched towards Moore's Creek Bridge in 1776 and for those who had not, 1777 brought pressure, largely occasioned by the establishment of a permanent state government and its militia. Men between the ages of sixteen and fifty years were required to muster in their neighborhoods, and those who had not taken the oath of allegiance to the state were required to take it on mustering day. After April, 1777, it was a new oath. The one used after Moore's Creek Bridge was worded vaguely enough to shield a tender conscience:

> I A.B. do sincerely promise and swear, that I will be faithful and bear true allegiance to the State of North Carolina, and to the Powers and Authorities which are or may be established for the Government thereof, and that I will to the utmost of my Power, maintain and defend the same against all Attempts whatsoever; and I do swear, that I will do no act wittingly, whereby the Independence of the said State may be destroyed or injured. SO HELP ME GOD.[26]

The new oath, embodied in the state's first treason act, allowed no mental hedging:

> I will bear faithful and true allegiance to the State of North Carolina, and will to the utmost of my Power, support and maintain, and defend the independent Government thereof, against George the Third, King of Great Britain, and his Successors, and the Attempts of any other Person, Prince, Power, State, or Potentate, who by secret Arts, Treason, Conspiracies, or by open Force, shall attempt to subvert the same, and will in every Respect conduct myself a peaceful, orderly Subject; and that I will disclose and make known to the Governor, some Member of the Council of State, or some Justice of the Peace, all Treasons, Conspiracies, and Attempts, committed or intended against the State, which shall come to my Knowledge.[27]

The law directed that this oath be offered to crown officials and merchants trading directly with Britain; they could take it or give bond to leave the state within sixty days. It could be administered to anyone, however, and it came to be used with the militia even before a law specified that it be offered to every adult male.

Demands to take the new oath and muster with the revolutionary militia forced public decisions. George Redman, a citizen of Rowan County, left a partial account of such a muster when he swore a deposition against John Depoynster and Joseph Hendricks. On the day appointed for oath-taking in their militia district, Redman noticed a "number of persons" behaving "in a riotous manner" who withdrew a short distance from the main group. Since the militia captain was busy administering the oath, Redman and a few other men went to see what "the rioters" were doing. He found Depoynster and Hendricks "dissputeing about the black Jack which was a nicname they gave the Oath of Aleigance." Hendricks accused Depoynster of "swallowing

I Stephen Conger Adjutant to the
1st No Carolina Battalion —
do acknowledge the UNITED STATES of AMERICA to be Free, Independent and Sovereign States, and declare that the people thereof owe no allegiance or obedience to George the Third, King of Great-Britain; and I renounce, refuse and abjure any allegiance or obedience to him; and I do Swear — that I will, to the utmost of my power, support, maintain and defend the said United States against the said King George the Third, his heirs and successors, and his or their abettors, assistants and adherents, and will serve the said United States in the office of Adjutant — which I now hold, with fidelity, according to the best of my skill and understanding.

Sworn to before me this
15th day of May 1778
Lach. McIntosh B.G. Stn Conger

Oath of Allegiance

the black Jack," Depoynster denied it, and when Depoynster convinced Hendricks, "they drank friends together [and] with a great Shout Horawed for king George the third."[28]

Similarly outspoken against the "black oath" was James Glen of Surry County. He took the oath but later declared that it was "Contrary to his Conscience" and that "a time would soon come when the sons of Liberty would be obliged to take as many Black Oaths contrary to their conscience." Glen refused to pay his taxes, allegedly forcing a distress of his property so that he "woud have a Receipt ... in order to shew General Howe that he Disapproved of the measures carried on . . . ."[29]

Some sought to avoid the dilemma by fleeing. William McQueen of Anson County went to the Pee Dee area of South Carolina and worked as an overseer because he had heard that overseers there would not be drafted. After five months he lost his job for refusing to cooperate with the local militia. Others fled to Indian lands or British areas.

New York was a haven for people near the coast. The wealthy Halifax merchant Archibald Hamilton and several of his relatives bought a ship in New Bern which they took to New York laden with North Carolinians who had refused the oath. Likewise, neighbors accompanied Flora MacDonald. Her husband sent a ship from New York following his exchange there as a Moore's Creek Bridge prisoner. Neil Snodgrass left North Carolina "in a very small crazy Boat which happily brought him to New York." He had been a merchant in Pasquotank County for twenty years.[30]

Sometimes oath and draft resisters banded together for protection or plunder. In Currituck County, Francis Williamson's house was a refuge for such "outliers." There were reports of tories rendezvousing, eating, and casting bullets at Williamson's. One witness reported that Williamson told Josiah Phillips, a leader of outliers along the Virginia border, that they must waylay the revolutionaries ("the shirtmen") and kill them, or else be killed by them. The witness rented land from Williamson. He had been a member of Phillips's group at the time. Another informant accused Williamson of talking in favor of Britain but also noted that Williamson was critical of the outliers. A trustee for two Anglican churches, Williamson was heard to say that the tories should stay in their own county "and not come in this to disturb the people here, that it was not decent for them to go to places of worship in the manner they did & that it ought not to be suffered."[31]

Recruiting for outliers and other groups offered curious possibilities. Perhaps no plan was more enterprising than John Clifton's scheme in southeastern North Carolina. Benjamin Morris related that Clifton tried to get Morris "to Join him to Raise an Arme of men in behalph of the King and . . . he said he would apply to the Congress for Money to Raise men." Clifton allegedly told Morris that he had a "constitution for them [recruits] to sign in behalph of the King and that he Rote to his farther Not to Let his too sons in the Regular Sarvis for he had found out a better way."[32]

Conspiracy: the gourd patch tories

Both Francis Williamson and John Clifton were on the fringes of a conspiracy for resisting the state oath and the draft which arose in several eastern counties just as the state's first constitution was being implemented early in 1777. Apparently it originated in the mind of John Llewelyn, a Martin County justice of the peace.[33]

Returning home from a muster in March, 1777, Llewelyn lamented to his two companions that there was a danger that "popery" would be imposed. He indicated that he had a plan for opposing it but needed his thoughts put on paper. One of his companions was James Rawlins, a preacher whose way with words Llewelyn evidently admired. Rawlins afterwards described this occasion as the beginning of the conspiracy. A few days later, Llewelyn and his son William called on Rawlins and the three of them composed a "constitution" which would be presented to potential recruits only after secrecy was insured.

Along with Llewelyn and Rawlins, James Sherrard of Martin County and Daniel Leggett, a Tyrrell County tailor, initiated at least about ninety recruits. A potential recruit was approached with the question: will you stand up for the Protestant religion? If the person answered in the affirmative, the danger to the religion was explained and a second question was posed: can you keep a secret? On answering "yes," the new man took an oath to keep secret what was about to be revealed. After administering the oath the recruiter might show or read the constitution to him. Then the recruit would be asked to take a second oath to support it. Should he decline, he would be reminded of his oath of secrecy. If the recruiter were someone other than Llewelyn, Rawlins, Sherrard, or Leggett, he would not disclose the constitution but would explain a sign and passwords and send the man to one of the four for the remainder of the initiation.

The constitution bound the members to oppose the state oath and the draft, to support Protestantism, and to keep on hand one-half pound of powder and two pounds of lead. Other aims of the group were mentioned by participants when they later gave information about it. It is difficult to know whether they were part of the written constitution or were simply the subject of common talk among the group.

When members later referred to the group as a "religious society," they were not inventing a term to deceive their examiners. With the 1776 constitution the Anglican church lost the privileges it had formerly enjoyed as the colony's established church. Even during its establishment, the Anglican church had been painfully short of ministers. One of the aims of the Llewelyn group was to obtain a reader and perhaps even a minister. When one potential recruit balked against taking the first oath, Rawlins assured him that their aim was to obtain an Anglican reader. At least one recruiter offered, in addition to the constitution, a subscription to a fund to hire a reader. When Leggett told a potential recruit that the group intended to have ministers eventually, the man exclaimed that he would contribute £5 if they would obtain ministers. At least two men became aware of the group at "a preaching." Each was invited to attend by one member and privately informed of the conspiracy by another at the meeting. The oaths were commonly taken by kissing the *Book of Common Prayer*, though several initiates seem not to have known what "the book" was. The name "senior warden," used for a person authorized to show the constitution, was taken from the terminology of the Anglican church. The sign and passwords had religious significance. The sign was a stick with three notches, and the passwords were "Be True" and "INRI," spelled alternately by the novice and the initiated. Several members mentioned a belief in the Old and New Testaments as a part of their constitution.

Fear and resentment aroused by disestablishment of the Anglican church were important in the Llewelyn conspiracy. The conspirators perceived the changes that were occurring in public life as dangerous to their religion. One of them later explained that he had thought the state oath "was very bad and would ruin his Sole."[34] While it was common talk that the new government would force people to worship images, it was not only the fear of France and Catholicism that made the independent, non-sectarian, state seem evil; it was tainted with atheism. In explaining to potential members the need for such a group, Leggett said he understood that several members of congress "had damned the Being of a God."[35] A commonly expressed grievance was that some thirteen or fourteen members of the provincial congress did not believe in the Trinity. The conspirators feared that the new state, having hauled in the Anglican anchor, might either drift into atheism or be towed by the French to a Catholic establishment. Both possibilities were rendered unlikely by the 1776 constitution's prohibition of office holding by anyone who denied a belief in either the Bible or the Protestant faith. If the conspirators were aware of this provision, it was not enough to allay their fears. Perhaps their perception of the new government was determined by the premise that treason against the king was akin to blasphemy against God.

The political orientation of the conspiracy was dominated by Llewelyn's animosity towards Martin County revolutionaries, in particular two militia captains and four justices of the peace. Llewelyn spoke of killing them for their threats to arrest him as a tory. Other conspirators referred to the revolutionary leaders as "the gentry" or "the gentlemen." They commonly said that if the king conquered "the gentlemen," the conspirators would keep their own estates and share "the gentlemen's" estates with the king's troops.

The conspiracy included several prosperous men. Property tax valuations for a sample of about 15 per cent of the known conspirators range from £100 to £17,402. Excluding the two highest valuations, which are clearly beyond the range of the others, the mean valuation is £1,181.11 and the median is £720. Several of the members owned slaves. Perhaps political and economic rivalry motivated some of the conspirators to oppose the revolutionaries.[36]

All the men who later gave information about the conspiracy concurred that it was designed to assist those who did not want to serve in the revolutionary militia. They spoke of aiding "persecuted" and "oppressed" men whom some of their neighbors called "tories." While it was understood that their opposition to independence was the justification for their draft resistance, politics was not their only consideration. Many of them denounced the draft for interfering with their farming schedule. Their depositions mention opposition to drafting "in crop time" as a goal of the conspiracy. It is possible, of course, that the qualifying phrase was invented or at least emphasized as a distraction after the revolutionaries discovered the conspiracy.

It was assumed that the group would make contact with Howe in New York. Some thought he already "had a hint of Matters." Llewelyn and Rawlins intended to go to Howe and inform him of their proceedings, but they got only as far as Scotland Neck before they ran out of money and returned home.

With one notable exception, the conspirators saw their military role as a passive one: they would organize and be ready to help a British force whenever it came. The exception, in which they were to take the initiative without waiting for the British, was Llewelyn's scheme to seize the Halifax magazine and Governor Richard Caswell. The plan was never executed; Caswell did not go to Halifax when they expected him. Llewelyn proposed that they encourage a slave insurrection to draw the revolutionary soldiers away from Halifax before they attacked. He wanted one of the conspirators who was a slave patroller to stage the slave revolt. It is almost certain that some of the members of the group did not know about this plan. Those close to Llewelyn were aware of his insistence that they should murder "the gentlemen" at night if the conspiracy were discovered. Sherrard, according to an independent witness, was so despondent about Llewelyn's intentions that it affected his behavior.

Of the approximately ninety known members of the Llewelyn conspiracy, a minimum of fifty-five men had at least one relative in the group; one family contributed eleven members, but they were exceptional. Most of the men were from Tyrrell, Bertie, and Martin counties. The most distant known adherent was from Anson County, and he joined the conspiracy while in Bertie County. Leaders boasted that one-half of the Fifth North Carolina Continental Regiment were sympathizers. The members told each other that their network extended to "South Carolina, Haw River & in short to all the Southern part of the Continent." Some of them mentioned "New Georgia" as the southernmost extension. Llewelyn said the plan arose in Virginia, but this probably was an attempt to distract from himself as its originator. According to Rawlins, after the conspiracy broke Llewelyn said if he were captured he would say that he got the plan from Rawlins who got it from a "Traveling Man."

The first person known to have given information about the conspiracy to revolutionary officials was the man whom Llewelyn had picked to cause a slave uprising. Perhaps this suggestion was too much for the slave patroller, who remained active in the group even after informing. The information he and a relative gave on June 4, 1777, was not very damaging. Between them they said that the organization agreed to oppose the draft "in crop time" and to rise if popery were introduced. There was no mention of a slave revolt, the Halifax magazine, or killing gentlemen in the night.[37] This may account for the revolutionaries' slowness in rounding up other conspirators.

More harmful information was disclosed by William May, Junior, on June 19. He said the group intended to refuse the state oath and the draft and to rescue forcibly any member who might be taken for resisting. Next day, the revolutionaries arrested William Tyler, the only man May had named. Tyler had papers regarding the conspiracy in his pocket. That night Llewelyn convened some of the conspirators at a gourd patch, which was their regular meeting place. They intended to take May and got powder from Daniel Southerland, a loyalist merchant in Tarboro.

As Llewelyn's talk became more irresponsible, some of the conspirators volunteered information to the justices of the peace, and others turned state's evidence following their capture. Rawlins was one of the last to be taken. He fled with his family from Martin County to Lake Mattamuskeet but was recognized in his sailboat and captured during the first week of August. Rawlins shared with the authorities a great deal of information about the conspiracy, and there is no indication that he and most of the other informers were criminally charged. Many of them yielded both to the state oath and to militia service.[38]

Such leniency must have disappointed any revolutionary who thought the new regime should make an example of the conspirators as a means of establishing its authority. Allen Jones, who had an exaggerated notion of the danger posed by the conspiracy, wrote from Halifax that it was

> a plot in favour of the British Tyrant. It was to have broke out with the assassination of the leading men in every county, and afterwards none were to be spared but such as repaired to their Standard—Heaven Blasted the Design .... I make no Doubt but hanging about a Dozen will have exceeding good Effects in this State & give Stability to our new governments [.] They seem to me to have been designed for this purpose by providence.[39]

In November, Leggett, his father Absalom, and Tyler were convicted of misprision of treason on the grounds that they were carrying intelligence to the enemy. Apparently the papers on their persons distinguished them from other conspirators. Misprision of treason was punishable by confinement and confiscation of one-half of one's property.

Llewelyn was found guilty of treason soon after the conspiracy was discovered, in September, 1777. His wife and several prominent men in Martin County (including at least two against whom Llewelyn had directed the conspiracy) petitioned Caswell for his pardon. On the recommendation of the Council of State, the governor granted a reprieve until the meeting of the General Assembly.

When the General Assembly met in November, the House suggested that the entire body vote on the pardon, but the Senate, emphasizing the separation of powers doctrine, refused to touch the issue. The General Assembly therefore told the governor that the original sentence of execution should have been carried out in the absence of any statement of mitigating circumstances from the judge who presided at Llewelyn's trial. They recommended that Caswell send orders to Edenton jail for Llewelyn's careful confinement until the date of the execution.[40] Apparently Llewelyn's wife aroused the sympathy of the Edenton District judge, John Baptist Beasley. He gave her "distressed circumstances" as his reason for stepping forward in Llewelyn's behalf two weeks after the General Assembly's decision. He could cite no mitigating circumstances other than the following: "I am so unhappy to have nothing to plead in his behalf but Mercy ... this much I can say that when he had an opportunity to escape out of Edenton Gaol he did not."[41] That was enough. John Llewelyn outlived the Revolutionary War.[42]

Llewelyn's personal animosities are the most obvious aspect of his own loyalist stand. For the men who found his conspiracy attractive, several other factors are evident. Opposition to the draft and the state oath was essential. At least for some, the desire to improve and protect the Anglican church was basic. As for the fears that independence would lead to French control, Catholicism, or atheism, they suggest that a significant number of people were confused and frightened by the political changes that were rapidly being made by men other than themselves.

Accommodation and defiance

The wide variety of people who were loosely classed as "tories" before the British invasion of the state forced firmer delineations included the wild men who ignored all authority and probably always had.

Henrey Daniel said he recognized no law, since British authority had vanished and the new government was not legitimate. He declared his own independence before the Rowan County justice of the peace to whom he was brought as a vagrant. When asked why he had no pass, Daniel "answered that he would not Seek for any Such thing from any of their Rulers." Questioned about the oath of allegiance, he replied that "he would not take it [and] he hoped god would keep him from the marke of the Beast nor would he Defend their Cause for he never had justice Done him from the States." Then Daniel threatened that if he were forced into the Continental Army, "he would Shoot the first officer that would offer to command him ... [and] if he was taken By any arbetrary power So that he would Be a Sufferer he would take the Life and the Lives of all and every such person and they might Depend on it and also that he was not a subject of the united States nor under its Laws nor ought its Laws to have any Concern with him."[43]

Many men who took the oath and served in the revolutionary militia would join the British forces in 1780. Thereafter, many of them would be considered loyalists by their neighbors, the British government, themselves, and posterity.[44] Some of them would boast that they only took the oath and mustered, refusing to march with the revolutionary militia when war actually came to their vicinity. Still others cheerfully served in the militia as long as the enemy was the Cherokee on North Carolina's frontier. In some areas prior to 1780 it was possible to pay a fine for not mustering, without attracting much attention to oneself.

That course often was taken by people who wanted to be neutral. In Rowan County a community made up largely of Germans attempted neutrality. During 1774-1776 the Rowan County Committee of Safety treated them gingerly but failed to coax them into making some statement of approval. Apparently many of them did nothing to break the 1777 treason law until they circulated and signed a statement of neutrality in 1778. In January, 1779, eight of them, having been arrested, acknowledged that they "signed a certain paper (which is now lost) purporting that they were for peace &c and would not take up Arms either for or against the States of America and ... [that] they meant not to hurt or Injure the American Ind[ependence] openly."[45]

Circulating a statement of neutrality could be construed as speaking or writing against the public defense, which was one of the actions constituting misprision of treason. The eight men were not charged, however, and when they went to court in March they simply gave recognizance of £400 each "to be of good behavior toward the state" for a year.[46]

The charge of speaking against the public defense was an easy one to make. The word of one witness was sufficient for an arrest and charge, if not for a conviction. The following examples are from the backcountry in 1778. They may reflect exaggeration and personal animosity, but they show some of the opinions and concerns of the accused persons. Land, money, taxes, and religion: these were the subjects about which they were angry enough, usually with the prompting of alcohol, to make statements which got them into trouble.

Land and taxes were on Elijah Lyons's mind when his tongue became loose in a tavern in the presence of James Dickey, who later informed on him. According to Dickey, Lyons declared that "our Assembly had no Right to open ye Land Office & that if any man would Molest him or take away his land he would shoot him." Dickey reminded him that he did not have the power to disobey the General Assembly. Lyons replied that he could raise men in twenty-four hours. Lyons concluded by proclaiming that "it was Damned Liberty to take our money when they had no Right & there would be other Laws in ye Land before long." The following morning Lyons went upstairs to Dickey's room and asked him to disregard their conversation of the previous evening.[47]

Anger that a revolutionary militia leader had entered land that was occupied prompted a conversation between James Forbis and one Spears. John Haggen overheard it and reported to a justice of the peace. Forbis was a blacksmith, and while he was working for Spears the latter complained that John Johnston had made a land entry for the land where Spears lived and had declared that he would not take £500 for his claim to the land. According to Haggen, Forbis tried to console Spears by telling him "of ye great faits of Lord howe & said that fifty of hows lite hors had drave Nine hundred of generl washingtons men." Haggen challenged Forbis, and they quibbled over the fighting to the northward. Forbis got the better of the argument until Haggen reminded him that he had taken an oath which forbade such talk. Then, according to Haggen, "Forbush answard & said that Nothing Never Consemed him so much as takeing that oath."[48]

Jacob Seits disdained the new currency in terms for which William Cathey informed on him. Cathey declared that he heard Seits "Say god Dam the Liberty money and them that made it for it was good for nothing and them that made it was good for nothing and he would tell them so before their face and he wished that they were in hell flames Burning."[49]

The currency was one of Richard Perkins's complaints as he drank and talked in Tryon County. Joseph Cronkleton later said that he asked Perkins if he had taken the oath of allegiance. According to Cronkleton, Perkins declared repeatedly that he had not and would not. Then Perkins took out "a bill of our New Emission ... and asked how much it was, and said Damn the Money for he Did not know what it was good for — and Damn the presperterians and Covenanters for they ware the Cause of this Desturbance ...."[50]

Jesper Smith in Anson County was another tory-tongued taverngoer. Thomas Jenings said he saw Smith give a bill to a tavern keeper "& said heare is a half dollar made by the damd Tories at Hallifax will you give any thing for it." The tavern keeper sold Smith whiskey for the money, whereupon, according to Jenings, Smith "drank to some of the Company

George King's Good helth. They askt what George King; he Answard King George."[51]

In December, 1778, a few months after Jesper Smith's indiscretion, King George's troops established a southern beachhead in Georgia. Their presence inspired hope of rescue and revenge in men like Smith. Such high spirits were evident as a group of Tryon County men who had refused to muster headed for Georgia early in 1779. A revolutionary leader said they "forceably Marched of plundering and Robing and taking prisoners as they went Bosting themselves that They would soon be victors after joyning the King's forces." They took horses and saddles from those who refused to join them. One such victim reported the group numbered more than one hundred men; later victims said the tories told them they were over three hundred strong. They outnumbered and defeated a party of revolutionary militia sent to collect men who had refused to muster.[52]

In Savannah incoming North Carolinians joined a new provincial corps, the North Carolina Volunteers. Their leader was John Hamilton. A nephew and partner of Archibald Hamilton, he had joined the British forces in New York and with at least thirty other North Carolinians under his command accompanied the British move to Savannah. Hamilton raised men in Georgia and sent recruiters into North Carolina. Groups of recruits were targets for interception. One group was captured on their way to Georgia and taken to "the Bull Pen . . . a place Built by the Rebells for the reception of Torries" near Augusta.[53] After transfer to Orangeburg they broke jail and reached Savannah in July, 1779. Another group left North Carolina in February, 1779, were captured, and spent ten months in a Charles Town prison ship before escaping to Georgia. Some people went to Georgia without knowing about Hamilton's corps and joined it once they were there. Daniel McNeill, having refused the oath twice in 1777, hid about in North Carolina and Virginia until the autumn of 1778. Hearing that the British were moving south, he went to Georgia and joined them at the first of the year. Later he raised a company of North Carolina Volunteers.[54]

II. WAR AND LITIGATION

Military service

Statements made after the war by men seeking compensation from the British government for their losses as loyalists indicate that the coming of British forces to the Carolinas in 1780 was a major turning point in their wartime experiences. Men who had avoided militia service by fines and stealth faced mounting pressure which flushed them into overt identification with British arms.

In Cumberland County, the heightened loyalist visibility seems to be reflected in an increase in the number of tax penalties levied by the revolutionaries in 1780. There inhabitants were assessed threefold and fourfold property tax for 1) refusing to submit an inventory, 2) refusing to take the oath of allegiance, and/or 3) refusing military service. (The 1778 tax law allowed Quakers, Dunkards, Mennonites, and Moravians to pay a threefold tax in lieu of military service, but the number and identity of persons so assessed in Cumberland County suggest that many of them were not penalized for religious reasons.) In 1778, 5 per cent of the assessed inhabitants bore such penalties; they constituted 10 per cent of the tax payers in the districts where any penalized persons lived. In 1780, penalized inhabitants made up 26 per cent of the county's tax lists, or 33 per cent of the taxpayers in districts reporting penalties.[55]

Cumberland County loyalists had received attention from the revolutionaries since 1776, but for some loyalists elsewhere, 1780 brought the first pressure. Jonas Bedford, for example, after the war said that he had suffered no "persecution" before the summer of 1780. Then, he said, the revolutionaries took 300 head of cattle from his home west of the Catawba River in Tryon County. A native of New Jersey, Bedford was a justice of the peace before the war and was elected to the original committee of safety for Tryon County. He did not serve. How "loyal" he was before 1780 is uncertain. There is only his statement — questionable because he made it in a compensation claim — that the revolutionaries took his cattle because of his known preference for the British. Soon thereafter he joined the loyalist militia being trained by Colonel Patrick Ferguson in the Carolina backcountry.[56]

After the British took Charles Town in May, 1780, the action in the South shifted to the backcountry. The British thought that the majority of the South Carolina backcountrymen would step forward to man their posts and turn in any neighbors who still harbored rebellion and that loyalists would assist British entry into North Carolina. The British mistake in South Carolina was to make their presence felt too strongly. It was hard to avoid. Patrick Ferguson, who understood backcountrymen better than any of his comrades did, identified the dilemma. He asked his commander, General Charles Lord Cornwallis, how to proceed without either "damp[en]ing the zeal of our friends" or "exasperating those rebels who are quietly disposed."[57]

British policy exasperated lukewarm revolutionaries and many neutrals as well. There never had been strong government in the backcountry, and the state government had made few demands on the inhabitants. Except for the people who did not want to take a state oath or perform militia duty, the people had not been greatly inconvenienced by the Revolution. The British occupation was more immediate.

The most offensive policy in the occupation was announced by General Sir Henry Clinton in June, 1780, before his return to New York. In effect, his proclamation said that all South Carolinians must take an oath of allegiance or be treated as rebels. Earlier, Clinton had tacitly recognized neutrality as an alternative. People who might have remained neutral while British authority was being restored went openly into opposition.[58]

A further cause of distaste for the British occupation was the spirit of fighting epitomized by Lieutenant Colonel Banastre Tarleton and his British Legion. In one of the early forays into the backcountry, Tarleton's men massacred some surrendered opponents at the Waxhaws. It won the British no friends. Thereafter, "Tarleton's Quarter" was the excuse for similar atrocities by the revolutionaries, and the fighting took on some of the characteristics of a blood feud. Vengeful loyalists were eager to participate. They and their revolutionary counterparts gave credence to earlier characterizations of backcountry society as violent and lawless. The civil war that accompanied the British occupation made life harder for the average backcountryman than it had been before the British came, and he heartily wished them gone.

Such were the circumstances in which North Carolinians joined the British forces in South Carolina and during Cornwallis's march through their own backcountry. For people who had lived through four years of

Henry Clinton **Banastre Tarleton**

persecution or sporadic exile, the British brought deliverance. Others took the oath of allegiance to the crown and joined the loyal militia because, as they admitted later, they expected the British to win the war. Very likely there were men who became "loyalists" because their personal enemies were on the other side. For a few weeks after the British entered the South Carolina interior, the area was quiet and people coming into the outposts to make their allegiance known took little risk. But from mid-June through August the revolutionaries took the offensive in a series of skirmishes which undercut the confidence of the scattered British installations and made loyalty a risky course of action.

The revolutionary offensive followed a loyalist assembly at Ramsour's Mill in Lincoln County, North Carolina, in June. Cornwallis had sent Lieutenant Colonel James Moore of the North Carolina Volunteers home to prepare loyalists to join Cornwallis when he should arrive. Moore brought the news of the British restoration in Charles Town. Hearing that the revolutionary militia was gathering nearby, Moore assembled about 1,300 loyalists at the mill with fewer weapons and no organization. Most of the men who thereby reestablished their allegiance have been characterized as "artless Germans, industrious, frugal, and honest citizens, who had never been in arms before or suffered persecution from the Whigs."[59] The revolutionaries attacked, much confusion followed, and both sides dispersed. When Moore reached safety at Camden, he had only thirty men with him. The battle encouraged revolutionaries to challenge the British position and aroused anxiety among other loyalists who were far from the British posts.[60]

Moore's rising and the revolutionaries' activities forced the hand of some British sympathizers who were not protected by nearby forces. Colonel Samuel Bryan led such a group from the Yadkin River to the Cheraws soon after Ramsour's Mill. Many of Bryan's men were from the area between the main Yadkin River and its South Fork, where loyalism and neutrality had been outstanding from the beginning of the conflict. Bryan and many of his men had turned out for the Moore's Creek Bridge campaign, although some of them had not lasted until the battle. Afterwards they lived quietly until the hard pressed revolutionaries drafted them into their militia in 1780. Rather than serve or go to jail, more than 810 men gathered under Bryan and headed for Cornwallis's army. The unit remained with Cornwallis until Yorktown.[61]

Andrew Hamm was one of Bryan's men. Hamm was born in Pennsylvania of German parents who seem to have settled in Rowan County in the 1760s. He lived on Abbotts Creek and had a sawmill and a grist mill. Captured in his attempt to join the loyal forces in the Moore's Creek Bridge campaign, Hamm remained inconspicuously at his home until the British took Charles Town. In the ensuing pressure for more militiamen he refused to serve against the British and led over 100 of his neighbors to join Bryan.[62]

A somewhat similar story belongs to three brothers from Mecklenburg County: Peter, Jacob, and John Blewer (or Bluer). They were born of German ancestry in South Carolina. In 1776 John signed the Association, but Peter refused and was threatened with imprisonment. The Mecklenburg County Court in 1778 ordered Jacob and John to explain their refusal of the oath of allegiance, but there is no indication that they were actually brought to court. On being drafted, they went to Camden and served as loyalist militiamen in South Carolina for the remainder of the war.[63]

While a number of North Carolinians travelled more than a week to reach the British, most joined after the forces reached their home areas. There were never as many recruits as the British, who long had received glowing reports of southern loyalists, expected. Cornwallis did not hide his chagrin at the paucity of volunteers between Guilford Court House and Wilmington. A few days after Guilford Court House he was on Deep River expecting former regulators to join him. He complained that "many of the Inhabitants rode into Camp, shook me by the hand, said they were glad to see us, and to hear that we had beat Greene, and then rode home again; for I could not get 100 men in all the Regulator's Country to stay with us, even as Militia."[64]

Lord Cornwallis

Most of the volunteers became militiamen. Patrick Ferguson succeeded in shaping the men of the Carolina backcountry into creditable fighters. He was impatient for action and got many of them, and himself, killed at King's Mountain, but he led them well, and they fought well.

The most dramatic militia coup was performed by two groups of North Carolinians working together after Cornwallis's departure: more than 500 Highlanders from Cumberland and Bladen counties and at least 50 men from Randolph and Chatham counties. In September, 1781, Colonel Hector McNeill of Cumberland County and Colonel David Fanning of nowhere in particular led them in an attack on Hillsborough. They rescued loyalist prisoners and captured over 200 men, including Governor Thomas Burke and his council. The militia were operating under the authority of Major James Craig, whom Cornwallis had left in command at Wilmington.[65]

The British used the militia extensively for noncombat functions. Knowing the country, they were useful as foragers, scouts, messengers, and spies. Militia leaders with high social standing were authorized to administer oaths of allegiance. In general, however, the militia served the regular forces in menial capacities, with waggoning, hauling, digging, and cattle-driving the most common assignments.

Militiamen realized that the regular forces considered them inferior. In turn, the militia were contemptuous of British errors that were caused by ignorance of the local situation. These attitudes were articulated by Robert Gray, a militia colonel from Cheraws District, across the South Carolina boundary. Gray shared with the regular forces the distinction between British and colonials and proudly counted himself in the latter category. His annoyance arose from a common British attitude that loyalists were little better than rebels. He blamed this assumption for the loyal militia's poor record in comparison with that of the revolutionary militia.

In particular, Gray contrasted the treatment of militia prisoners of war. When the Continental forces took militiamen prisoners he said they turned them over to the revolutionary militia, who punished or freed the prisoners on the basis of personal knowledge of them. Gray said that the loyal militia, by contrast, had no voice in the disposal of revolutionary militia prisoners. He complained that the regulars could not distinguish among men whom they did not know and tended to free all of them to make fresh attacks on loyalists' families. He did not understand the conciliatory policy of the British and saw only that it prevented their having a large supply of prisoners who might have been exchanged for captured loyalists. As a result, Gray maintained, the loyalist, if he did not choose to retire within the posts, a ruined Refugee [,] either joined them [the revolutionaries] openly or gave them private intelligence of the movements of parties for which he enjoyed real protection & was safe to go to sleep without danger of having his throat cut before morning. Had our militia been certain of being treated as prisoners of war by the enemy, many more would have sided with the royal Standard.[66]

Apparently revolutionary commanders vacillated between treating captured militiamen as traitors and as prisoners of war, depending on the prospects of a prisoner exchange. Colonel William R. Davie, mulling over the problem, observed that if considered traitors, their only "crime" was militia service for a king whose sovereignty they still acknowledged. Following the battle of King's Mountain, Colonel Martin Armstrong, misinterpreting his instructions, turned over his Surry and Burke County prisoners to the district court, thereby regarding them as traitors. He did so, he said, at the request of the civil officers and to prevent their being slaughtered as prisoners of war by some of his men. He explained, "Many of the officers from The other Side of the Mountain threatened that if the Tory prisoners were Taken to the westward they would raise a body of men & kill every one of Them."[67]

Plundering and requisitioning, sometimes barely distinguishable, came to loyalists, revolutionaries, and neutrals with the civil war in the Carolinas. The narrowness of the distinction between plundering and prudence can be seen in an order from the state Board of War to the Orange County Light Horse. The board forbade plundering, yet it told the men to "disarm all that are suspected of being Tories & undue care should be taken to remove such horses as will make Dragoons from the neighborhood of the enemy especially from those that are our enemies."[68] The military command on both sides issued orders against plundering but were aware of its persistence. In Rowan County some revolutionary militia officers were charged with attacking and plundering peaceful people on the accusation that they were loyalists. The Board of War directed General John Butler in Salisbury to help the civil magistrates bring them to justice.[69]

The fighting offered opportunities to settle old scores and to rob without regard to the victim's politics. Merchants were obvious targets. In Chowan County some men who had been driven from their homes allegedly robbed selected merchants because of their "oppression in trade."[70] Personal enmity was apparent in Mark Allen's attempt to get men to join him in attacking Richard Randle and Christopher Christian of Montgomery County. One whom he approached said later that Allen sought to form "a

Guard against the Tories As the Sd Allen had particular business to Settle of his Own with ... Randle and Christian."[71]

The Board of War tried to regulate the disposal of livestock, crops, and other food left behind by people fleeing either to join or to escape the British. They ordered county officers to take the food in both cases and make it available to revolutionary forces. If the goods had been abandoned by persons joining the British, enough food was to be left for the support of any women and children who remained. If the owners had fled to escape the enemy, "friendly" persons might obtain food for themselves after paying the specific tax on the goods.[72]

Both sides were desperate for soldiers. The chances were strong that a captured loyalist would become a revolutionary soldier as the price for his pardon, and vice-versa. Often the revolutionaries pardoned captured loyalists on condition that they join the state militia or the Continental Army. Such a reversal was deemed especially suitable for men whose only transgression was service in the loyal militia, but it was not restricted to them. Continental service had been a form of punishment for criminals since 1777. In a typical arrangement, two men were convicted of treason and two of felony in Hillsborough and were sentenced to die; each was allowed to earn a pardon by serving in the Continental Army for a year. Similarly, the Craven County court meted out Continental service to loyalists and hog thieves alike. Apparently it was brotherly affection that got John Abbott out of Halifax jail, where he was held on suspicion of treason, and into the Continental Army. His brother Richard promised that John would serve for three years if released; should John be unwilling to serve, Richard agreed to serve in exchange for John's release. In Nash County, a company of the Nash Light Horse took John Evans to the courthouse and threatened to hang him immediately if he refused to enlist for eighteen months. After meeting their demand, Evans asked what crime he had committed to merit such vigorous recruiting. His captors replied that he had been thinking about joining "the Insurgents in Edgecombe."[73]

Dr. John Pyle was an outstanding loyalist who was forgiven by his neighbors. He was a native of Chatham County and a regulator. Pyle and his son John fought at Moore's Creek Bridge, were sent out of the state as prisoners, and returned to Chatham County. In December, 1776, he took the mild oath of allegiance and gave bond before the provincial congress. Early in 1781 Pyle responded to Cornwallis's call to arms by raising three or four hundred men between Haw River and Deep River in Orange and Chatham counties. They headed towards Hillsborough, expecting to rendezvous on the way with an escort of Tarleton's British Legion.

Instead they met a smaller group of revolutionaries under Lieutenant Colonel Henry Lee and Brigadier-General Andrew Pickens going in search of Tarleton's party. Mistaking the revolutionaries for Tarleton's men because of the similarity of some of the uniforms, the loyalists drew to within eyeball range of their enemy, who had recognized them on first sight, and were overcome in the ensuing ten-minute skirmish. At least one hundred of Pyle's men were killed; Pyle and many others were wounded.[74]

The identities of twenty-eight of the loyalists who survived the fight can be conjectured from Chatham County court records. In May, 1782, there were thirteen civil suits against groups of men which included known adherents of Pyle at the battle. The defendants totalled twenty-eight men; fifteen of them were named in more than one suit.[75] Family ties are apparent in the fact that thirteen of the twenty-eight men can be accounted for by four surnames. About seven of the men, including John, William, and Samuel Pyle, went to the Charles Town area after the battle and were either in the militia or provincial corps there, but Pyle and his son John surrendered to a revolutionary militia officer in the autumn of 1781.[76]

Pyle's medical skill smoothed the way for his reacceptance in spite of his long record of opposition to the Revolution. He treated wounded American militia on at least three occasions. When Pyle's treason trial convened in November, 1782, the jury found him not guilty, and he spent the remainder of his life in Chatham County. Later in that court session, practically the same jury acquitted three other men accused of treason. Land records and the 1790 census indicate that at least twelve of the twenty-eight men, in addition to the Pyles, were living in Chatham County after the war.[77]

The loss of property

In every year from 1776 through 1782 the state legislature passed laws providing for the confiscation of loyalist property. Reflecting the turmoil amid which they were framed, they are a mass of legal contradiction.[78] Some of the legislation was suspended during the height of the fighting. Initiative for the disposal of loyalist property lay with the county and district commissioners of confiscated estates, and the county and district courts determined whether or not an accused person should be included in the application of the various laws.

The operation of the confiscation laws was not the only way in which loyalists lost property. The property of absentees could be attached for debt and trespass. It was easier to prove that an absconded man was a debtor or had committed trespass than it was to convince a jury that he had taken action encompassed by the confiscation laws. In the case of a small landowner with little movable property to satisfy the debt or trespass charge, the effect was the same: his land was sold at public auction.

If the circumstances of the war and his participation in it allowed a loyalist to remain on his land after the British withdrawal, and if it were not sold before the Act of Pardon and Oblivion was passed in 1783, his chances of keeping it seem to have been good. Thereafter a confiscation trial would involve the question of whether the accused was encompassed in the Act of Pardon and Oblivion.

The act denied pardon to several categories of people: 1) those who had borne British commissions, 2) persons named in the confiscation laws, 3) people who had left the state with the British and had not returned for a year prior to the passing of the act, and 4) individuals guilty of murder, robbery, rape, or houseburning. The act specifically denied pardon to Peter Mallet, David Fanning, and Samuel Andrews.[79] In general, the Act of Pardon and Oblivion did not benefit loyalists who had left North Carolina and relieved those who had remained, for the circumstances of the war and the British withdrawal made it likely that men to whom the exemptions applied would have fled with the British anyway.

Of the twenty-four men in Wilmington District who were indicted for treason in the Superior Court during 1782 and 1783, seventeen were present. They pleaded the Act of Pardon and Oblivion during their 1783 trials. The court judged that they were encompassed by the act and freed them. Even Peter Mallet was acquitted in a trial that lasted almost all day and for which twelve prospective jurors were challenged. In 1785 and 1786 Mallett's right to sue in North Carolina courts was questioned, but again the court found in his favor on the basis of the 1783 decision.[80]

Sometimes departing loyalists attempted to circumvent confiscation in the hope that they would be able to return soon. Such ruses as conveying one's land to a relative usually did not work. They were expressly voided by the 1781 confiscation law. Conveyance to a friend was less likely to be detected, but it could prove embarrassing or dangerous to the friend. A more elaborate stratagem was for a friend to claim a debt on the absent loyalist's property and thereby receive money from its sale.[81]

Whether by the oversight of county officials or by his own artifice, Peter Blewer managed to sell his Mecklenburg County land after living several

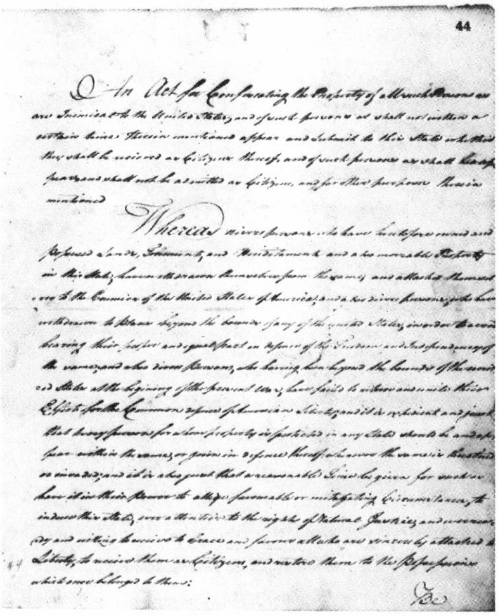

Confiscation Act

years in British territory. Blewer bought the 178 acres in 1774, but he did not register the deed. He moved from Nova Scotia to South Carolina by 1790, when he sold the land for ten shillings more than he had bought it. The 1774 transaction was registered three months after the registration of the 1790 sale, a fact which suggests artifice.[82]

The 1782 confiscation law provided that wives and children could retain household goods and enough land to support themselves, but the compensation claims contain too many tales of families being driven from the land and onto the charity of friends and relatives for this provision to have been regarded as anything more than a suggestion. Families of men condemned to execution by the Hillsborough District Court for joining Cornwallis in 1781 were allotted a bed and a cow each from the condemned man's property. In the case of absent loyalists whose property was taken to satisfy a debt or a trespass charge, there was not even the law's guideline. James Hamilton of Rowan County, who had served in Samuel Bryan's militia, owned no land, but he had registered an entry for a tract. In 1781 the commissioners of the confiscated property took a slave and thirty head of livestock. About the same time a man from whom he and another loyalist had taken horses and weapons during the war sued the estate for £125. To satisfy the suitor the court attached these goods from Hamilton's wife:

twelve head of cattle, five hogs, two beds with bedding, five pewter plates, three pots, a chest, a dough trough, a loom with tackings, and the tract of land Hamilton had entered. Hamilton was with the British forces near the coast at the time. Apparently he did not return to Rowan County; he was living in his native Ireland in 1783.[83]

Loss by debt: the trials of Mary Dowd

Another Irishman whose family suffered from actions of debt recovery was Connor Dowd. His family had more to lose than Hamilton's, and their fight to keep it illuminates a part of the loyalist experience.

Dowd was a linen bleacher before he came to America to seek his fortune in 1754, bringing only some linen that his mother gave him. He was a peddler in North Carolina until he married a woman who owned 500 acres. Dowd's complete illiteracy seems not to have handicapped his business transactions, and he became a wealthy merchant and planter in Cumberland County, with a luxurious home, a tannery, a distillery, a tavern, and bolting and grist mills. Shortly before the Revolution began, he extended his operations into Chatham County. Between 1774 and 1777 Dowd bought 450 acres on Deep River and the creeks feeding it, where he built a store, a grist mill, and a ferry on the main road between Hillsborough and Cross Creek.[84]

Dowd provided supplies for the loyalists before Moore's Creek Bridge. Later he said he had provided osnaburg, linen, bed tick, iron, gun flints, shoes and shoe leather, saddles, bridles, wagons, flour, pork, beef, venison, and rum. Captured after the battle, Dowd was freed on £1,000 bail. The following August he still flaunted his disdain for the revolutionaries. The Council of Safety ordered him to sell his salt supply, about 110 bushels, to revolutionaries who had fought at Moore's Creek Bridge. The officer delivering this order reported that Dowd "peremptorily refused."[85] After the war Dowd said the plundering of his property began in 1776. In 1777 his arrest for "treasonable practices" figured in a political rivalry between two revolutionaries even though Dowd was reputedly on the verge of taking the state oath.

When Cornwallis came through his part of the state, Dowd raised a force of about forty mounted men. After the war he said that Cornwallis's leaving had prevented their joining his force. They were active in the fighting that followed Cornwallis's departure, and thirty of them, including Dowd's son, were killed in the campaign surrounding Burke's capture. Afterwards Dowd found it necessary to slink to safety at British-occupied Wilmington. After the Cumberland County revolutionaries seized and sold his property he went to Charles Town and from there to England in August, 1782, where he sought government compensation for his losses. Dowd had left his wife and ten children in Chatham County.[86]

In November, 1782, the Chatham County court confiscated Dowd's property. At first they allowed his wife and children one-third of his estate for their maintenance. In view of the large family, the court allowed them "the whole part of the Estate" which he had possessed in Chatham County.[87] The vague wording allowed questions to arise shortly. Were they to keep all his land in Chatham County or just the tract on which they lived? Was the possession to be limited to her lifetime? Could the children inherit the land? Could it be sold? Did his "estate" include movable property and debts?

Mary Dowd had difficulty collecting her husband's debts. A family friend introduced a bill in the General Assembly which resulted in an act enabling her to sue for his debts in her own name.[88] Thereafter she became a very litigious lady, but not a remarkably successful one.

Mary Dowd expected her husband to return home. She went all the way to the governor to determine his status under the Act of Pardon and Oblivion. A loyalist who had returned to North Carolina wrote to his father, an exile in Britain: "Mrs. Dowd waited on the Governor to know if Mr. Dowd sou'd be allowed to come back who told her that Mr. Dowd was looked upon as a good Member of Society & would have no objection to his return."[89]

Dowd returned to North Carolina in 1783. One assumes that he brought with him some British trade goods for which there was such high demand after the war. He bought almost 1,500 acres of Chatham County land from the state during 1783 and 1784 before returning to Britain. Whatever his intentions were, the land served as a financial cushion for his family, for either Dowd neglected his creditors during this brief stay, or the debts charged against him over the next few years were false.[90]

Persons claiming to be Dowd's creditors sued for debt recovery in the county court. When payment or sale of movable goods was insufficient to meet a debt, the law provided for the sale of real estate. From 1785 through 1789 three tracts of Dowd's land totalling 842 acres were sold by the court in this way. One sale was of mill sites which had served as security when Dowd purchased cattle for the British or loyalist forces. In addition his wife sold 450 acres in three tracts to pay his debts during this period.[91] In 1786 a returned loyalist wrote to Dowd in Ireland that the county court had ordered the sale of the family home on Deep River and that his wife was barred from his other lands. Of Dowd's family, the friend said, "It is absolutely Necessary you come over as soon as possible to their relief otherwise they must disperse." He added, "Only those of the country that will swear a Debt whither true or false will get any property arrested & sold as my Lands & Catle were sold for a Debt that never existed [Patrick] Traverse &tc &tc made fortunes by this trade & John Cox a member of assembly."[92]

Possibly an urgent plea from his wife brought Dowd back to North Carolina. In January, 1789, she wrote, "the miscarriage of your letters has occasioned several of your old friends to take such advantage of the little I had to support the children, that unless you can be here yourself, I shall be reduced to a truely deplorable condition."[93] If he returned that summer, he seems not to have remained long, for the 1790 census includes her as the head of the household, and subsequent litigation is in her name. In 1789 either he or she completed the purchase of 710 more acres of Chatham County land from the state which had been entered in his name earlier. They were not to keep it.[94]

A few weeks after the land was bought the General Assembly passed a second law concerning Mary Dowd. There is no indication that she requested this one. The 1784 act in effect had given statutory authority to her possession of his estate as reserved by the county court. The petition for the 1789 bill said that she was unable to pay Dowd's debts without selling the land, yet there was some doubt regarding the legality of her sales of his land. The new law protected the purchaser against claims of either of the Dowds or their heirs.[95]

Over the next ten years, Mary Dowd sold more than 1,000 acres in a piecemeal manner suggestive of reluctance. During this time she lived in Moore County, the part of old Cumberland County where they had lived before moving to Chatham County. In addition to her sales, the county court sold three tracts, so that by 1800 the Dowds had lost almost all their land.[96]

The final blow came in 1800 with the court-ordered sale of 500 acres on Bear Creek which had been bought in 1789. The sale ended a decade of legal maneuvering by which Mary Dowd tried to save the tract.

In 1788 John Beck (or Berk) of South Carolina, a former neighbor, declared that Dowd owed him £250. Unable to sue for the debt in the district court, Beck moved the matter to the Chatham County court. The suit was tried in November, 1790, but resulted in a hung jury. Beck sued again in May and won. When Mary Dowd contested the judgment she was overruled. Her next defense was to have the guardian of one of her children sue Beck for trespass: evidently Beck had collected the money or its value in goods. Meanwhile, she appealed the case. In May, 1792, the county court upheld its original judgment in Beck's favor, and she took her cause to the district equity court. There both of them received a hearing, but at this point the matter all but disappears from the extant records. The only litigation noted further is her 1794 suit against Beck in which she was assessed £10 damages. The issue evidently continued, for she filed an appeal. The court's sale of the 500 acres to satisfy Beck's debt attests to her failure.[97]

Dowd was in Chatham County during 1803. His mother died early that year and bequeathed him part of the money from the sale of her estate. His final land sale, in 1803, refers to him as being "of Chatham County." In it he sold his remaining 100 acres to the trading company that had bought some of his mill sites, his store, and adjacent land.[98]

Some other litigants

Many men in Dowd's position who had left with the British and whose property was confiscated chose either to seek compensation from the British government for their losses or to try to regain any unsold part of their property. Not everyone had a choice; some men because of financial or physical limitation faced only one possibility. Either choice was a gamble, but available evidence indicates that they preferred to regain even a part of their land. Indeed, London encouraged this choice.

To obtain compensation they had to prove that their property had been confiscated and sold. Such proof was best obtained from a county court. Subtle decisions had to be made by the loyalists and by friends who worked for them: if the court certified that an estate had been confiscated, certainly there was no chance that the same court would restore any part of it.[99]

Daniel McNeill's future was unpredictable when he returned from Nova Scotia to North Carolina in December, 1784. He hoped to remain. If that were not possible, he wanted to collect some debts and obtain proof of the confiscation of his property with which to fortify his compensation claim. A native of Cumberland County, McNeill had been a fierce commander of raiding parties during the height of the civil war, and he was not welcomed home. He barely escaped a New Bern mob and two "country" mobs and landed in the Wilmington jail on a misdemeanor charge. His misdemeanor was to re-enter the state. The jury that indicted him made it clear that they thought the mercy provisions of the Act of Pardon and Oblivion should not apply to him. He was released on paying a £10 fine and giving £500 security to leave the state within sixty days. McNeill was successful in obtaining proof of his property loss, so the trip was not in vain.[100]

Similarly, a 1784 attempt by Alexander McAuslan to collect debts brought out a New Bern mob. McAuslan had been in New York, Newfoundland, and the West Indies since the war ended. Unlike McNeill, he eventually resettled in North Carolina. Some time between 1787 and his death in 1791 he returned and resumed his mercantile activities. He was living in Chatham County at the time of his death.[101]

It was not always possible to obtain proof of confiscation even if a loyalist had a friend working for him in North Carolina. James Gernon asked John Maclellan of Wilmington to get certification of his losses in Hillsborough and Salisbury judicial districts. Gernon had been a merchant and an Indian trader before the war, and Maclellan had worked for him from time to time. In 1786 Maclellan wrote Gernon that he had been unable to go to Hillsborough and Salisbury; he had been told his life would be in danger if he tried to enter the backcountry. "And as for Obtaining a certificate from the county court," he said, "I might as well obtain absolution off the Pope of Rome."[102]

The Irish heirs of Matthew Colvill, who had been killed at his Bladen County home in 1781, hired Archibald Maclaine to try to save some of Colvill's confiscated property. A Wilmington lawyer, Maclaine worked for several loyalists. In May, 1783, Maclaine wrote the heirs "that upon his appearing at the County Court to set aside the confiscation . . . he was attacked by a Mob with drawn Swords, wounded by them and with difficulty escaped from being assassinated." Two years later Colvill's nephew went to North Carolina and tried to recover the unsold part of the land. By 1788 he fled to Virginia after hearing that if he remained, "he might expect his Uncles fate."[103]

III. THE EXILES

Although there were loyalists leaving — and returning to — North Carolina throughout the war, the largest exodus was in 1781 and 1782. Many who voluntarily joined Cornwallis on his march through the state had little choice but to remain safely with the British forces after the tide of war turned against them.

Apparently the most bitter internecine strife began after Cornwallis's departure. It persisted even after Major James Craig's forces, whom Cornwallis left behind at Wilmington, withdrew to Charles Town following the news of Yorktown. Some loyalists who did not leave with Craig were driven from their homes and fled to Charles Town. There during 1782 they could risk returning to their homes and the wrath of their neighbors or resign themselves to remaining with the British when they evacuated Charles Town in the autumn. Some of the men had been accompanied by their families when they left North Carolina. For a few, particularly officers in the militia or provincial corps, a truce would be arranged for them to go home for their families. Such a trip was dangerous. The wives of some officers in the North Carolina Highlanders returned to their homes under a flag of truce to get their children. They were imprisoned for seven weeks, but they eventually reunited their families in Charles Town.[104]

When Cornwallis left Wilmington, fewer than 100 North Carolina provincial troops and some militia went with him. About 350 provincials evacuated with Craig to Charles Town. They were in three units. The largest, the Royal North Carolina Regiment, dated from John Hamilton's 1779 recruiting from Savannah but was composed largely of men who had joined Cornwallis's advance. The North Carolina Highlanders harked back to Martin's commissions before Moore's Creek Bridge. They had revived in 1780-1781. A third corps, about thirty-five dragoons, were the Independent Company of North Carolina Volunteers. In the Charles Town area the North Carolina Highlanders became part of the Royal North Carolina Regiment under Hamilton's command. They carried over 400 names on the roll in June, 1782, but there were only about 300 men present.[105]

In addition to the provincial corpsmen, about 500 North Carolina militiamen went to Charles Town. Over 100 men arrived in 1781. Most of them were in the British withdrawal from Camden, where their number had been reduced by smallpox. About 400 North Carolina militiamen joined them on James Island after the evacuation of Wilmington. Some of the militia who continued to fight in the interior after Craig left Wilmington went overland to Charles Town. David Fanning and men who had fought with him reached the city in the spring. Probably the last North Carolinians to reach Charles Town were sixteen prisoners exchanged in October, 1782. They were provincials and militia.[106]

Their extant correspondence and known activities suggest that most of the loyalists who left North Carolina considered it home and wanted to return. Many of them did. Meanwhile, they were temporary or permanent exiles in Britain, East Florida, the West Indies, the Bahama Islands, and areas that now are three Canadian provinces: Nova Scotia, New Brunswick, and Ontario. Movement from one of these places to another was not uncommon.

Loyalist dispersion is well illustrated by the post-war activities of the Samuel Williams family of Anson County. Williams raised a company for the Moore's Creek Bridge campaign. He fled to Georgia with his four sons after the defeat. They moved to the loyal colony of East Florida in 1778, and Williams commanded a company of a provincial corps there in fighting along the Georgia border. Williams and his sons Henry and Jacob fought in the Georgia backcountry after the British re-entered that colony and ended the war at Savannah, where Henry's wife and seven children joined them. From Savannah they and another son, William, returned to East Florida in the British evacuation. By this time one of Jacob's legs had been shot off and smallpox had blinded one eye; his father was totally blind. The fourth brother, Samuel, Junior, ended the war in New York in the Barrackmaster General's Department.

They never got together again. Samuel, Junior, went to New Brunswick in the British evacuation of New York, and in 1792 he settled in the newly opened lands of Upper Canada. The father died prior to 1787. Henry and William went to the Bahama Islands in 1784 and were planters there for several years. Henry probably returned to Anson County, for in 1807 a Henry Williams owned land near the family's pre-Revolutionary home. Jacob made his way to London in search of compensation, but like many other loyalists he was too poor to pursue it effectively amid the red tape of legal London and the aggressive multitude of other compensation-seekers. He died in a London workhouse.[107]

British Evacuation of New York

In London

The administrator of the Mary Le Bow workhouse in which Jacob Williams lived and died commented that "he is at times perfectly in his Senses."[108] Insanity was a common affliction among displaced loyalists in London, and the North Carolinians were not immune. The American Loyalists Claims commissioners, who by parliamentary authority screened applicants for compensation, believed Ann McLeod to be "not in her right mind." She was the widow of John McLeod, whom she did not see for seven years after his capture at Moore's Creek Bridge until shortly before his death in Jamaica. Their six children were with her in London. One wonders if Donald Morrison's jump from a second story window in which he fractured his skull is completely explained by the fever he mentioned in connection with the incident. Anguish over his financial situation prompted the former Halifax merchant Alexander Telfair to shoot himself at Liverpool, where he was trying to resume his business. He had filed a claim for £3,578 and needed most of it to pay his debts. After four years the claims commissioners recommended he be given £522 and paid his first installment, £126, which precipitated the suicide. His wife was a native of America and had no relatives in Britain. She moved to her mother-in-law's home in Scotland. The loyalists frequently commented that Britain was strange to them and that the hardships they bore as refugees in London were at least as unpleasant as their wartime captivities.[109]

Usually the refugees remained in London only long enough to pursue compensation. Most of them received slightly less than one-third of the estimates of their losses. They supported themselves in the metropolis famed for its harshness to country bumpkins. Daniel Southerland's skill as a tinworker obtained him employment in Westminster. Elizabeth Bridge helped support her ill uncle, formerly a merchant in Halifax, by her work as a milliner's apprentice. Jane Stenhouse told the claims commissioners she had been a schoolteacher in Cross Creek and was skilled in "milleneray, mantua making, shroud making and every branch of needlework." In view of the adroitness with which she had hidden loyalists following the battle of Moore's Creek Bridge and had escaped an order for her arrest, it is unlikely that her hands were idle in London. She lived near Carnaby Market. Joseph Rathell tried to make money from his American hardships. The Dublin native had lived for fifteen years in America until his nocturnal trip to the New Bern liberty pole in October, 1775. He wrote a manuscript about America but was unable to find a buyer among the London booksellers and printers. One of them told him that the public was saturated with writings about America.[110]

The North Carolinians kept in contact with each other in London. In seeking compensation they needed acquaintances to attest to their deeds of loyalty and especially to verify their property and losses. At least fifteen of them lived in the vicinity of Clerkenwell Close, an area also inhabited by some South Carolina and Georgia loyalists. Contact with friends in North Carolina was commonly made through Scottish and Irish merchants. Recipients of letters from the exiles sometimes complained that they had been opened and read all along the route, and even purposely delayed, but such eighteenth century practices were by no means limited to the mail of loyalists.

In East Florida

North Carolina loyalists who went to Britain usually did so to make claims or to join their relatives in Scotland or Ireland. As a place to start a new life, East Florida was far more attractive. Its familiar climate beckoned, and its nearness to North Carolina would make return easy, should the revolutionaries mellow. Virtually a new colony, East Florida offered hope after their defeat, in spite of the rumors that Britain would abandon it too.

In the evacuations of Savannah and Charles Town some 3,500 whites and 7,500 blacks went to East Florida, joining several hundred loyalists who were there already.[111] Southern loyalists tried to rebuild their lives in a fashion similar to what they had known before the war. They cleared and planted new land, took over St. Augustine, and dominated the assembly and colonial offices. A few months after their arrival they learned that Britain had ceded their new home to the Spanish. Responses included a feeling of betrayal, much bitter talk, and plans for uprisings in which North Carolinians played significant roles.

The St. Augustine garrison was manned by about 520 members of three southern provincial corps: the Royal North Carolina Regiment, the South Carolina Royalists, and the King's Carolina Rangers. Describing them shortly after the cession was announced, a St. Augustine resident wrote a friend in London:

> Our Troops are likewise very mutinous, a few nights ago several have been killed, their plan was to burn the barracks, plunder the Town, & take Possession of the Fort, and to arm all the Negroes, & to put every white Man to Death that opposed them keeping the Country to themselves as they will rather die than to be Carried to Hallifax to be discharged, how all this will end I know not but am afraid Mischief will be done as their spirits are not broke yet.[112]

The provincials figured in plans for a revolt. After news of the cession arrived, there was talk in the northern part of the colony of a rising to greet the Spanish on their arrival. The conspirators assumed that the British would recognize their *fait accompli* and rescue them if the Spanish tried to conquer East Florida. Three years later, witnesses said that 2,000 refugees and other East Floridians had been "ready to act" in 1783 and that the three provincial corps would have joined them. The plans were blocked by Colonel John Hamilton at the head of the Royal North Carolina Regiment. Refusing to command the enterprise, Hamilton threatened to oppose it, since in the first instance it would be directed against British authority.[113]

The hope of opposing the cession by force lived on, even after the provincials were disbanded or removed in the autumn. In the spring of 1784 evacuation orders arrived from London and ended the speculation that Britain might keep East Florida after all. Plans to prevent the Spanish from taking possession revived and became a threat to the peaceful transfer of power.

The plans surfaced under the leadership of John Cruden, a North Carolina merchant. Before the war Cruden, his uncle, and his brother had stores at Wilmington, Cross Creek, and Guilford County. During the British occupation of coastal South Carolina he rose to some prominence as "commissioner of sequestered estates" with authority from Cornwallis. His duties were to supervise the distribution of lands and slaves confiscated from the revolutionaries in the Carolinas. He was unable to control the distribution, but he took his position seriously. In East Florida Cruden made a nuisance of himself by trying to keep a record of the revolutionaries' slaves brought into the colony by the loyalists. Claiming still to be under Cornwallis's authority, he sought to return these slaves to their owners in the United States. He thought the laws banishing loyalists and confiscating their property would be rescinded as a result. Cruden's zeal was fruitless. East Florida's Governor Patrick Tonyn refused to sanction his attempts until after the confiscation and banishment acts should be repealed.[114]

Whatever Cruden's plans were, they were surpassed by those of his associates. Apparently Cruden intended organizing a force to overpower the Spanish officials when they reached East Florida. Some of the loyalist refugees were to go to North Carolina, South Carolina, and Georgia to recruit men for service under Cruden. He seems to have had correspondents there. His original plan was considered inoffensive by Lieutenant Governor John Moultrie, who refused a request that he be commander-in-chief of the undertaking but who kept the secret. Another member of the governor's council agreed to participate. On a false pretext, Cruden called mass meetings in the northern area of the province in order to ascertain the number of men available. At this point the enterprise fell apart. Some of the conspirators wanted to join forces with the robber gangs who were tormenting the north — perhaps they were the same people — and take over the government of East Florida *before* the Spanish arrived. This was to be accomplished by about 200 refugees in St. Augustine and more in the north. Plans were to overtake the garrison, ships, and fort at St. Augustine and capture the governor, the garrison commander, and other officials. Then a general assembly would be called, and a determined people would prevent the servants of His Catholic Majesty from taking possession.

A step was taken toward overthrowing the provincial government. A robber band attacked two detachments of regular troops from the garrison. They dispersed one detachment, killed the captain and one of the men, and captured the sixteen soldiers who manned a northern post. These attacks on His Majesty's troops were too much for Cruden; he offered his services to Tonyn to help put down the conspirators. The governor put him in charge of subjugating the robber gangs. He empowered Cruden to call out the militia for a *posse comitatus* and demand the assistance of the magistrates. In cooperation with the governor's civilian cavalry force, Cruden dispersed some of the thieves and executed one of them.[115]

When or how Tonyn learned of the conspiracy is not clear. Perhaps he learned of it when Cruden abandoned the project. Tonyn claimed to have had some knowledge of it earlier. Cruden's commission is dated May 26, 1784. On May 21 Tonyn prepared an undated document with which he planned to acquit the garrison commander of the crisis whenever meeting it head-on could be averted no longer. He requested the commander to capture and confine the leaders, whom Tonyn would name when he sent the notice. He did not find it necessary to send it. Apparently he told no one in the colony of the conspiracy. With the conspirators divided, and with the earnest Cruden pitted against the robber gangs, the governor waited out the situation. By the time the Spanish governor arrived in July, 1784, rumors of a loyalist uprising were widespread. Tonyn assured the new governor that the robbers, not Cruden's followers, were the danger. Tonyn considered Cruden a harmless eccentric. He told the Spaniard that Cruden's continuing hopes of East Florida's remaining British were "merely chimerical, and such as deserves no kind of serious consideration."[116]

Cruden and others persisted in their hopes. In October, 1784, as the "President" of "The British American Loyalists who took Refuge in East

Cruden became General of Sequestered Estates in Charleston.

Florida," Cruden petitioned Carlos III for autonomy under Spanish sovereignty for the northern area. He analyzed the loyalists' dilemma as follows:

> We may it please your Majesty are Reduced to the dreadful alternative of returning to our Homes, to receive insult worse than Death to Men of Spirit, or to run the hazzard of being Murdered in Cold blood, to Go to the inhospitable Regions of Nova Scotia or take refuge on the Barren Rocks of the Bahamas where proverty and wretchedness stares us in the face Or do what our Spirit can not brook (pardon Sire the freedom) renounce our Country [,] Drug the Religion of our Fathers and become your Subjects.[117]

Cruden's analysis expressed a common attitude. Neither of the choices was attractive. His little conspiracy delayed the evacuation of East Florida just as it was getting underway. In East Florida and in the Bahamas he performed increasingly strange and incoherent antics which suggest he had lost his sense of reality.[118]

In the Bahama Islands

Throughout the war the Bahama Islands had been a haven for loyalists, particularly from the nearby southern colonies. Coastal merchants and others with shipping connections found Nassau a convenient spot from which to redirect their businesses. At the end of the war they were joined by other refugees from the southern states, New York, and finally East Florida. While there were poor whites and free blacks among the new Bahamians, the most cohesive and influential newcomers were slave-owning southern refugees. Slaves were a relatively easy form of property to salvage, and the Bahamas, like the West Indies, offered the opportunity for employing them. Moreover, large areas of ungranted land in the islands seemed to offer the prospect of simulating their pre-Revolutionary societies.[119]

The wealthier of the southern loyalists in the Bahamas threw themselves and their resources into creating a cotton-based plantation economy. The fertility of the thin soil lasted only a few years. The best crop was in 1790, and productivity declined sharply even while more land was brought under cultivation during the following years. During the brief cotton boom, the planters built elaborate homes and introduced such cultural amenities as a newspaper, plays, and a lending library, while disdaining the way of life of the native Bahamians, whom they derided as "Conchs."

In the realm of politics, the new planter-merchant aristocracy clashed with Governor John Maxwell, who was not willing to share power with them. They organized a Board of American Loyalists, ostensibly to maintain loyalists' rights against the governor and the old inhabitants. Not all loyalists in the Bahamas identified with the group. Maxwell pointedly courted backcountry and New York loyalists to reinforce his and the Conchs' position. The governor's challengers were too much for him. The president of the Board of American Loyalists was James Hepburn, formerly a lawyer in Cumberland County and now a planter on Cat Island.[120]

The governor and the planters sparred over several appointments after Maxwell denied an audience to Hepburn, but the power struggle came to a head with the autumn 1784 election of an assembly. Disputes over election returns resulted in a walk-out by several loyalists and finally a prorogation. Maxwell was recalled to England, and a number of controversies raged between his faction and the Board of American Loyalists while the administration was in the hands of an elderly former Georgian, James Edward Powell.

For Hepburn and his allies, the perfect solution would have been Maxwell's replacement by one of their own kind. They asked London for a governor who had been a southern loyalist, and a North Carolinian was ready at hand. John Hamilton sought the office. He had taken land in Nova Scotia but had not settled there, and in 1788 and 1789 he took grants in the Bahamas. A group of southern loyalists, most of them North Carolinians, petitioned Secretary of the State Lord Sydney to appoint Hamilton governor of the Bahamas. Instead of getting a southerner as governor, the loyalists got John Murray, earl of Dunmore, the last royal governor of Virginia. Already he was an anathema to the planter group because of his 1776 offer of freedom to slaves who would serve with the British forces.[121]

It took the planter faction ten years to force Dunmore out of the Bahamas. The planters themselves gave up their Bahamian dream around the turn of the century, returning to the United States and leaving the islands to the Conchs and to the blacks and mulattos whose numbers they had significantly increased.

In Nova Scotia and New Brunswick

Except for a handful of militiamen who chose to go there in the evacuation of Charles Town, North Carolina loyalists approached Nova Scotia with great reluctance. Even the Scots, who might have identified with its name, were unenthusiastic. The loss of East Florida, with its warm climate and proximity to their homes, made Nova Scotia seem colder, more remote,

Tory Refugees on Their Way to Canada

and less pleasant than it really was. An East Floridian said of it, "[I] fear that it is to[o] cold for us to bear it now we have bin so Long in this hot climett."[122]

Their fears notwithstanding, North Carolinians took part in the loyalist influx to Nova Scotia and its offshoot province, New Brunswick. Like refugees from other colonies, many of them would not remain, but about 475 men, women, and children from North Carolina made new homes in Nova Scotia, and approximately 150 others settled in New Brunswick.[123]

About 150 of the men were in the Royal North Carolina Regiment. Upon their discharge they were given land with the King's Carolina Rangers and the South Carolina Royalists. Their settlement was at a cove near Country Harbour in the southeastern part of the peninsula. There were about 500 people in all, some 130 of them family members and slaves.[124] The five captains and many of the privates in the Royal North Carolina Regiment had service records dating back to Moore's Creek Bridge. Most of the captains had been taken prisoner then and had raised their companies upon returning south with the British forces. The group consisted predominantly of Scots from Cumberland, Anson, and Bladen counties.

Country Harbour was the largest southshore inlet in the eastern half of Nova Scotia, and large ships could navigate about ten miles inland. The provincial corpsmen built their settlement on the eastern side of the harbor, six miles from its mouth, at a place where the harbor was more than one-half mile wide. They gave it the disquieting name of Stormont. It was within fifteen miles of other loyalist settlements. Land near the site was stony and barren, but good land was available inland. The forests were superior, and many lakes abounded in trout. The settlers combined subsistence agriculture with lumbering and fishing.

There was a settlement of Scottish North Carolinians on the Musquodoboit River in Halifax County. The nucleus was ten men, four women, and two children who were there as early as May, 1784. Most of the men who have been identified were from Cumberland County and had served in the militia. Later they were joined by former North Carolina neighbors who had been to London or East Florida. The sizes of their land grants suggest that several more of the men were joined by their families. The provincial agent who distributed provisions to them as refugee loyalists in 1784 commented on the good fishing there and judged the place to be "a very promising settlement."[125]

Miles McInnes of Anson County was one of the Musquodoboit settlers. His compensation claim gives a glimpse of what must have been a typical wilderness experience. He said their group was the first white settlement in the area. The land was stony and full of underbrush, but fertile. The settlement was about fifty miles up the river, and communication with Halifax was by water and hazardous most of the year. When they first went in, they had to cut roads around three waterfalls. He said they missed the distribution of tools which the provincial government made to the loyalists. During their first winter they had to eat their seed potatoes, and by the time they got more from Halifax the following year the season was too far advanced for a successful crop.[126]

Some North Carolinians lived for a while at Shelburne, the loyalist center that changed from a boom town to a ghost town in a decade. In the southwest corner of the peninsula, Shelburne was one of the chief landing points from the New York evacuation. It teemed with refugees clamoring for provisions, implements, and land. Those loyalists who were accustomed to wealth squandered their remaining money building fine houses, opportunists seized what they could from government generosity, merchants brought goods to wharves they hacked from the wilderness, and blacks and poor whites gathered expectantly in huts and tents along the edges of the town. The governor of Nova Scotia was writing chiefly of Shelburne when he related that the peninsular settlers

> are now quareling and disputing among themselves, some selling their Lands and going to the United States, many from the States coming here, forming in the Whole a most Hetrogenious mixture of Loyalists and *pretended* Loyalty, different Sects of Religions (almost all sorts) disbanded Soldiers and Sailors of all Nations, several ships with Emigrants from Scotland and Ireland, Convicts, the sweepings of the Street of London sent by the Lord Mayor, near 3000 Negroes from the different parts of the Continent, some of them desperate Vilains, the tout ensamble a choice Sett.[127]

One of many merchants who tried to recoup his fortune at Shelburne and failed was Samuel Campbell of Wilmington. The business of Campbell and his partner, Robert Hogg, had a stormy existence during the war, and in 1781 Campbell joined Craig and left with the British. As colonel commandant of the North Carolina militia in Charles Town, he was the highest ranking of the refugees who went from Charles Town to Halifax in 1782. Campbell was in Shelburne by May, 1783, with his family and several slaves. He obtained a warehouse lot, a wharf lot, and fifty acres near the town, but he did not prosper. Campbell received some money from Hogg's brother in Wilmington, who had managed to retain some of their property. During the war Campbell had married Hogg's widow, and their son Samuel, Junior, was born in Shelburne in 1788. The son would sit in the Nova Scotia Legislative Assembly in the 1820s. Campbell seems to have died there, for his widow married Colin Campbell in Shelburne in 1792. Her new husband was a lawyer who had moved from Scotland to New York early in the Revolution.

At least twenty-five North Carolinians, most of them Scots, moved out of Shelburne to areas around the nearby Tusket and Jordan rivers. Several of them had their families with them.

Some North Carolina loyalists who lived for a while at Shelburne crossed the Bay of Fundy into New Brunswick. Others had gone there directly from the evacuation of New York, and still more reached New Brunswick after a stay in Britain or the West Indies. They settled along the rivers which empty into the Bay of Fundy and on the Miramichi River in the north. Many of them scattered, but two easily identifiable groups were the North Carolina Volunteers and the North Carolina Highlanders who evacuated from New York. The Volunteers, and perhaps also the Highlanders, went in company with the New York Volunteers. In 1784 the North Carolina Volunteers numbered seventeen men, three women, and five persons who were either servants or slaves. They settled on the Keswick and Miramichi rivers and in coastal Saint John County. In the summer of 1784 there were thirty-six people in a settlement of North Carolina Highlanders on the St. Croix River: sixteen men, ten women, and ten children. Later some of them moved to nearby St. Andrews; as its name suggests, it was a Scottish community also.

Black loyalists and Sierra Leone

More than 3,000 blacks accompanied the British forces to Nova Scotia and New Brunswick after the war. After about nine years, many of them participated in another exodus, this one to Sierra Leone. Some of the black loyalists were from North Carolina. While part of them were free at the beginning of the war, most seem to have been former slaves who had run away from their owners in response to their own misunderstanding of British policy.

As early as Dunmore's 1776 proclamation of freedom to Virginia slaves who would serve in the British forces, British military leaders had accepted the voluntary military service of runaways as well as free blacks. During the southern campaign, the British welcomed blacks in general—not just armsbearing men—into their occupied areas as a means of weakening the economy of the revolutionaries in the South. The British were not motivated by abolitionist sentiment; they merely were fighting a war. Nevertheless, a result seems to have been "an almost universal belief in slave society that a British victory would mean the eradication of slavery in America."[128]

Accordingly, thousands of slaves went behind British lines and remained until the end of the war. Then some of them participated in the British evacuations of Wilmington, Savannah, Charles Town, New York, and East Florida and so became part of the loyalist influx into Nova Scotia and New Brunswick. Other blacks went there as slaves belonging to white loyalists and British officers.

Once in Nova Scotia, several loyalist-owned slaves ran away. The presence of black communities made concealment easier than it had been in the former colonies. Freedom acquired in this manner was not secure. In addition to the danger of being identified by their owners, escaped slaves were liable to capture and sale by persons trading with the West Indies. The Halifax and Saint John newspapers carried advertisements for runaway slaves, most of them subscribed by Carolina and Georgia loyalists shortly after their arrival. As late as 1792 John Agnew of Maugerville, New Brunswick, gave notice that his man Prince had absconded for the third time. Agnew perhaps came from Hertford County, North Carolina, by way of East Florida. In describing Prince, Agnew listed what must have been the best part of his own wardrobe:

> He carried off with him a new grey cloth coat with short skirts, and a lapelled waistcoat with trowsers of the same, all neatly made, and mounted with metal buttons—also a new surtout coat of a lighter grey, with metal buttons and long skirts—a new fox skin cap with a bushy tail, and a good hat—three good shirts—one of them of very stout linen—a pair of good shoes, and a pair of new grey and purple coloured stockings, and a very good blue and black cloth coloured coat, mounted with silk chequered buttons, rather too large for him.[129]

Four slaves escaped from Thomas Hamilton of Country Harbour, formerly a captain in the Royal North Carolina Regiment. Using a warrant obtained from a justice of the peace who was a former resident of Charles Town, Hamilton seized them in Halifax, intending to take them to the Bahamas. Hamilton's vessel stopped at Shelburne, however, and the blacks appealed to a magistrate there who freed them.[130]

A separatist identity developed within the black communities. It was nurtured by the blacks' second class status in their new home and a fundamentalist religious revival which contributed the main outlines of their new identity. They came to think of themselves as a chosen people called out of slavery to a Promised Land. So far, however, the land was no more than a promise.[131]

Blacks who had served in the British forces had been promised land grants on the same scale as those of white loyalists. The governors of Nova Scotia and New Brunswick were instructed to grant land to black and white loyalists impartially. Nevertheless, the basic grant for a white private without a family was one hundred acres, and the most a black received was forty acres. The vast majority of the black men received no land.[132] Land was a prerequisite for the independence and security the blacks had sought in becoming loyalists. The hope of obtaining land inclined many of them to respond favorably to a scheme for settling free blacks in Sierra Leone.

The plan was devised by British philanthropists organized as the Sierra Leone Company. The company grew out of Granville Sharp's work with poor blacks in London and aimed at discouraging the slave trade while increasing other forms of trade between Britain and West Africa.

In 1787 the company sponsored a settlement, mainly of free London blacks, but its destruction by an African king increased the company's need for potential colonists. Sharp was aware of the blacks in Nova Scotia and New Brunswick through the sponsorship of black schools there by another philanthropic group to which he belonged.[133] The plans of the Sierra Leone Company became known in Nova Scotia and New Brunswick in connection with complaints by blacks living there concerning their land allotments. The blacks' spokesman was Thomas Peters.

Peters was from the Cape Fear area of North Carolina. He left his owner in 1776. His wife, also a former slave, was from the Charles Town area.[134] He was a sergeant in a black provincial corps, the Guides and Pioneers, and went to Nova Scotia with the corps and their families on the evacuation of New York. Most of the Guides and Pioneers learned that they would receive only twenty acres each instead of the one hundred acres they had been promised during the war. To make matters worse, a deputy surveyor mistakenly laid out their lots in school and glebe reserves. In addition, the Guides and Pioneers were offended by the pettiness of a provisions distributor. Representing them and about one hundred free black families in New Brunswick whose lots were eighteen miles from their town, Peters went to London. There he petitioned the home secretary for new and better grants; he probably had met Sharp when he made the petition.[135] In it he said the blacks preferred to remain in Nova Scotia and New Brunswick but were willing to settle on any British land.

Peters responded favorably to the Sierra Leone plans, and Home Secretary Henry Dundas gave the Sierra Leone Company permission to recruit settlers among the free blacks in Nova Scotia and New Brunswick. The company would supervise the settlement, with the government providing transportation and provisions for the settlers. The company chose John Clarkson to direct the emigration and a Halifax merchant and Quaker, Lawrence Hartshorne, to assist him. Each settler would receive twenty acres with ten additional acres for his wife and five for each child.[136] Dundas instructed the governors of Nova Scotia and New Brunswick to assist Clarkson.

In acquainting Governor John Parr with the company's plan, Dundas stressed that the move was to be voluntary and that those blacks who were satisfied in Nova Scotia or New Brunswick could choose to remain. After initial hesitation, Parr did not act on the secretary's implication that Clarkson need not be enthusiastically assisted. Nor did he heed the wishes of Shelburne whites, who valued the blacks for their cheap labor.[137] The governor and his Halifax-dominated council encouraged the migration. Haligonians could only profit from the commercial aspects of the undertaking, for the ships were provisioned at Halifax. Parr's only fear was that so many blacks would leave that he and the province would look bad. Neither he nor the New Brunswick officials cooperated with Peters in his recruiting efforts.

About one-half of the people who went to Sierra Leone were from Birchtown, the black settlement adjacent to Shelburne. In November, 1791, 518 Birchtown inhabitants agreed to go: 151 men, 147 women, and 220 children. Approximately one-fourth of these men had been born in the Carolinas.[138] One of the residents, a Baptist preacher, described the recruiting in the Birchtown-Shelburne area.

> The next fall [1791] Agent (afterwards Governor) Clarkson came to Halifax, abouting settling a new colony at Sierra Leone. The white people of Nova-Scotia were very unwilling that we should go, though they had been very cruel to us, and treated many of us as bad as though we had been slaves. They attempted to persuade us, that if we went away, we should be made slaves again. The brethren and sisters all round, at St. John's Halifax, and other places, Mr.

Wesley's people [i.e., Methodists] and all consulted what was best to do, and sent in their names to me, to give to Mr. Clarkson, and I was to tell him that they were willing to go. I carried him their names, and he appointed to meet us at Birchtown the next day. We gathered together there, in the meeting-house of brother Moses, a blind man, one of Mr. Wesley's preachers. Then the Governor [i.e., Clarkson, later Governor of Sierra Leone] read the proclamation, which contained what was offered in case we had a mind willingly to go. We appointed a day over at Shelburne, when the names were to be given to the Governor. Almost all the Baptists went, except a few of the sisters whose husbands were inclined to go back to New-York; and sister Lizze, a Quebec Indian, and brother Lewis, her husband, who was an half Indian ....[139]

The "official" explanation of why so many blacks left was that the climate of Sierra Leone was compelling. It also indicates that the Nova Scotia officials believed most of the people to have been southern slaves before the war. The council president reported to Dundas,

> The number [1,196] exceeded my expectation; but as they had come from the Southern Colonies, where they & their Children had been well Clothed & Fed by their Masters, into a Cold Climate; in which they were to depend on the Cultivation of the Country for their Subsistence, they readily embraced the Offer of going to a Warm Climate, with flattering hopes of a better condition.[140]

It does not appear that the provincial government compelled the blacks to leave; that they enticed them with descriptions of fertile soil and a pleasant climate is likely.[141]

The alacrity with which some of the provincial officials encouraged the migration should not obscure the fact that the blacks themselves were motivated to move to the new land. Peters had initiated the project and recruited colonists, and the black Baptist and Methodist churches had been focal points in its organization.

Once in Sierra Leone, however, white domination was as evident as it had been in North America. Upon their arrival in March, 1792, Clarkson learned that he was to be superintendent of the colony with a council of seven whites. The councillors soon made it clear that they did not regard the abilities of the blacks as highly as did Clarkson. This difference in attitude and the councillors' mutual jealousies handicapped Clarkson and eroded some of the trust with which the blacks regarded him.

Clarkson's task was awesome. Inadequate planning by the company in London combined with the unfamiliar climate to take a high death toll. Provisions were short after the first month, and the tents in which the blacks lived offered little protection against tornadoes and the long rainy season. Fever raged among the tents and aboard the ships where the whites were lodged. When the rain stopped in September, fifty-seven of the 119 white officials had died, and only about 1,000 blacks remained alive.[142]

Pressed by these and other problems, Clarkson asked the settlers to have their requests presented to him in writing rather than orally as in the past. At this point Peters became a focus of discontent, and there was talk of his replacing Clarkson. Clarkson regained control of the situation by calling a meeting of the settlers and asking them to choose between himself and Peters. No one chose Peters. Peters's final discredit came when he took money from a dead man. Peters said the money was owed to him, but an all-black jury reprimanded him. Peters gave the money to the widow and died soon thereafter. Sightings of his ghost were reported that summer.[143]

The black loyalist nucleus of the Sierra Leone colony survived and made distinctive contributions to African nationalism. Descendants of the black loyalists still maintain today their "creole" identity in Sierra Leone.[144]

In Upper Canada

From New Brunswick many settlers pushed on into Upper Canada, a new province created out of Quebec. Solomon and William Austin were North Carolinians who left their New Brunswick lands for better things further west. Solomon Austin had served in the Queen's Rangers under John Graves Simcoe, the post-war lieutenant governor of Upper Canada. Their acquaintance got Austin a good mill site in 1795.[145] Soon thereafter, at least fifteen other North Carolina families moved into Upper Canada, but apparently not by way of New Brunswick. Some of them had moved first to the Genesee lands on the frontier of New York, where they had "discovered as it were, that his Majesty had Territories of which they had not even heard."[146] One wonders, of course, how much of the motivation for leaving the United States so long after the war was a preference for British government and how much was land hunger.

The people whose North Carolina homes are known were from the backcountry. Almost all the men had done military service or had lost their fathers in loyalist service. They complained that they still suffered from the animosities aroused during the war. The Austins clearly began the little migration, followed by another family whose head had served under Simcoe, and then by men whom they had known in militia service.

A pioneer settler of Rowan County in the 1750s and a justice of the peace before the Revolution, William Spurgin was a consistent loyalist throughout the conflict. After the war, his wife struggled in the courts to keep some of his estate out of the hands of suitors. Apparently Spurgin returned to Rowan County, for tax lists include someone by his name in 1784 and 1785. This William Spurgin had been assessed £450 taxes in 1778. In 1784 he was listed as owning twelve slaves but no land. In 1785 he was listed as an insolvent. The 1784 and 1785 assessments may reflect confiscation, for Spurgin had owned six tracts and had sold only five of them prior to 1785. He sold the last tract in 1789. In 1785 William Spurgin and another returned loyalist[147] were convicted of horsetheft and sentenced to be hanged, but Spurgin was still living in Rowan County in 1790. A North Carolina loyalist named William Spurgin was in Upper Canada by 1796. He used the title "colonel" which the Rowan County former justice of the peace bore during much of the war, and the North Carolinians where he settled said they had known him in North Carolina during the war. He received 1,200 acres for his loyalist service, a generous allotment even in view of Spurgin's seven-member family.[148]

Another Rowan County immigrant to Upper Canada, and the last of the group to arrive, was a German whose name appears in English as Albright Spring. In 1795 he sold his Rowan County farm for £500, but he did not leave Rowan County until 1800 or 1801. He arrived in Upper Canada with his wife, seven children, an orphan, and some cattle in July, 1801. Early in the Revolution, Spring had had a brush with the committee of safety, and in 1778 he had paid a fourfold tax, but there is no indication that his land was confiscated, and there is no extant record of post-war legal difficulties other than a caveat suit he filed in 1784. When Spring applied for land in Upper Canada, he made no boast of military service. He simply said he had been a loyalist. With the paucity of information about the German family, one can only wonder if they left the North Carolina backcountry simply to find land on a newer frontier (Kentucky was nearer!) or if they had reason to say, as hundreds of other Americans who sought land in Canada claimed, that they were "desirous to exchange our Vassalage under the Republicans for the Liberty we formerly enjoyed ... under ... Great Britain."[149]

IV. CONCLUSION

The foregoing experiences of North Carolina loyalists suggest several observations. Taken altogether, the loyalists exhibited a coherent pattern of wartime activity. Their disapproval of the revolutionary course of events resulted in recalcitrance and grudging conformity before the test-administering committees of safety. When the opportunity arose, many overtly resisted the Revolution by joining the force that was defeated at Moore's Creek Bridge in February, 1776. The British failure to support adequately the counter-revolutionary rising, and Governor Josiah Martin's subsequent departure, forced opponents of the Revolution at least to acknowledge its reality. From 1776 until the British returned to the Carolinas in 1780, their responses to it ranged from accepting the state oath and mustering with the revolutionary militia to leaving the state to join the British forces. In 1780 and 1781 the nearness of the British facilitated overt opposition to the revolutionaries, and lines were drawn more clearly. With the British withdrawal and the end of the war, men who found themselves on the losing side could try to make peace with their neighbors or become refugees in some British area. Some of those who left returned to North Carolina later.

It seems that the most crucial period was the four and one-half years which followed Moore's Creek Bridge and preceded the British invasion. During that time, North Carolinians who had been less than enthusiastic about the revolutionary movement could adjust to the changed political situation and assess its impact on themselves. Their stands in 1780 and 1781 provide a more seasoned commentary on the Revolution in North Carolina than does the initial alignment in 1775 and 1776. The primary sources examined for the foregoing account give the strong impression that the number of North Carolinians willing to take a stand against the revolutionaries increased between 1776 and 1780. Approximately 1,000 North Carolina provincials and militia left Wilmington with the British in 1781. That figure does not reflect the service of 1) men who remained in North Carolina, 2) men who were serving outside the state in 1781, particularly in South Carolina, or 3) men who had been killed. Nor does it include civilian refugees. Likewise, an estimate of exiles after the war does little to indicate the wartime strength of North Carolina loyalists. Nova Scotia and New Brunswick, the only areas where North Carolina refugees have been studied, attracted approximately 625 men, women, and children. Considering their peripatetic nature, and excluding East Florida, one can conservatively estimate that at least that number moved to all other British areas after the war. The number of loyalists who left North Carolina during the conflict has not been determined, but there are indications that Scotland received a considerable number.

Throughout the conflict, North Carolina loyalists represented a variety of backgrounds; the segments of the population from which they were drawn produced revolutionaries as well. Even the conspicuous loyalty of many of the Highland Scots of the Cape Fear Valley was paralleled by the revolutionary stand of other Highlanders. In general the overriding issues appear to have been local, and some of them were of a family or personal nature. They were even more diverse than DeMond's pioneering work indicated; some regulators, for example, became revolutionaries, but others were loyalists.

Before the puzzle of why some North Carolinians took one stand while others much like them took the opposite position can be solved, local studies must provide some missing pieces. For example, backcountry land studies could disclose the impact of the state's land policies and thereby illuminate the complaints for which men like Elijah Lyons and James Forbis were considered tories. For the treatment of loyalists and their integration into the post-war society, local studies also are the key. Beyond the framing and content of laws, their application in the courts awaits further study.

ABBREVIATIONS

N.C.A. North Carolina State Archives, Division of Archives and History, Department of Cultural Resources, Raleigh

A.O. Audit Office Papers, P.R.O.

P.R.O. Public Record Office, London

S.C.A. South Carolina Department of Archives and History

P.A.C. Public Archives of Canada, Ottawa

P.A.N.S. Public Archives of Nova Scotia, Halifax

C.O. Colonial Office Papers, P.R.O.

S.H.C. Southern Historical Collection, University of North Carolina, Chapel Hill

NOTES

[1]I am grateful to Jerry Cashion for this information.

[2]Lawrence H. Leder (ed.), *The Colonial Legacy: Loyalist Historians* (New York: Harper and Row, 1971), 1-2.

[3]For bibliographic essays covering recent research relating to loyalists, see Robert M. Calhoon, "Loyalist Studies at the Advent of the *Loyalist Papers Project*," *New England Quarterly*, XLVI (1973); Robert M. Calhoon, *The Loyalists in Revolutionary America, 1760-1781* (New York: Harcourt Brace Jovanovich, 1973), 559-565, hereinafter cited as Calhoon, *Loyalists;* Wallace Brown, "The View at Two Hundred Years: The Loyalists of the American Revolution," *Proceedings of the American Antiquarian Society,* LXXX (1970), 25-47, periodical hereinafter cited as *PAAS.*

[4]William H. Nelson, *The American Tory* (Oxford: University Press, 1961 and Boston: Beacon Press, 1964) Beacon edition, 91.

[5]Calhoon, *Loyalists,* 85-105, 147-190.

[6]For an examination of the loyalists as conservatives, see Leonard W. Labaree, "The Nature of American Loyalism," *PAAS,* LIV (1944), 15-58.

[7]For a description, see Robert A. East, "The Loyalist Program" *PAAS,* LXXXI (1971).

[8]Minutes of the Rowan County Committee of Safety, Secretary of State's Papers, N.C.A., hereinafter cited as Rowan Committee of Safety.

[9]Shaw to Mrs. Shaw, May 25, 1778, Shaw Papers, N.C.A.

[10]Miller to Thomas Burke, December 12, 1774, Thomas Burke Papers, N.C.A.

[11]Miller to Burke, April 6, 1775, Thomas Burke Papers, N.C.A.

[12]Miller to Burke, April 6, 1775, Thomas Burke Papers, N.C.A.

[13]Miller and his family fled to New York during the war. He went from there to Bermuda and later to Charles Town after the British entered South Carolina. In 1782 he moved to East Florida, but the following year he was back in Charles Town applying for citizenship, for which several North Carolina revolutionaries recommended him. Miller died in Charles Town, and his widow got some of his North Carolina property restored to her in 1785. Their son James returned to North Carolina. Claim of Elizabeth MacNair, A.O. 12:37; Petitions to Senate, Confiscated Estates Papers, S.C.A.; Miller to Burke, March 26, 1783, Thomas Burke Papers, N.C.A.; Walter Clark (ed.), *The State Records of North Carolina* (Winston and Goldsboro: State of North Carolina, 16 volumes, numbered XI-XXVI, 1895-1906), XVII: 308-309, 371, hereinafter cited as *SRNC.*

[14]Minutes of the New Bern Committee of Safety, August, 1775, Secretary of State's Papers, N.C.A. For widely differing "tests," see Rowan Committee of Safety, November, 1775, and February, 1776, and Minutes of the Tryon County Committee of Safety, August and October, 1775, Secretary of State's Papers, N.C.A.

[15]William L. Saunders (ed.), *The Colonial Records of North Carolina* (Raleigh: State of North Carolina, 10 volumes, 1886-1890), X, 127-129, 182, hereinafter cited as *CRNC; SRNC,* XI, 768; Claim of James Cotton, A. O. 13:118; Claim of Jacob Williams, A.O. 13:124.

[16]Hugh Franklin Rankin, *The North Carolina Continentals* (Chapel Hill: University of North Carolina Press, 1971), 28-31, hereinafter cited as Rankin, *North Carolina Continentals;* Piers Mackesy, *The War for America, 1775-1783* (Cambridge: Harvard University Press, 1965), 44.

[17]Rankin, *North Carolina Continentals,* 31; Paul Hubert Smith, *Loyalists and Redcoats: A Study in British Revolutionary Policy* (Chapel Hill: University of North Carolina Press, 1964), 23, hereinafter cited as Smith, *Loyalists and Redcoats.*

[18]Smith, *Loyalists and Redcoats,* 26-28.

[19]Rankin, *North Carolina Continentals,* 28-54.

[20]*The New York Packet,* March 28, 1776, quoted in *SRNC,* XI: 290.

[21]Campbell to Thomas Burke, Cornelius Harnett, and John Penn, April 12, 1778, Thomas Burke Papers, N.C.A.; *CRNC,* X:559; *SRNC,* XI: 222.

[22]*CRNC,* X: 827-828.

[23]Neither of these men was a recent immigrant. Mercer was a Virginia native, and Ray's family had moved from Scotland in the 1750s when he was a year old. Both men settled in New Brunswick after the war but Ray returned to North Carolina prior to 1790. Fort Bragg now encloses his grave. Claims of Joseph Mercer and Daniel Ray, A.O. 12:35; Esther Clark Wright, *The Loyalists of New Brunswick* (Moncton, New Brunswick: Privately printed, 1955), 305, 321, hereinafter cited as Wright, *Loyalists of New Brunswick;* Petitions of Joseph Mercer, 1787 and 1796, New Brunswick Land Grants and Petitions, P.A.C.; Index to North Carolina Graves, N.C.A.; *SRNC,* XXVI: 460.

[24]Claims of James Cotton, Donald McCrumen, Soirle McDonald, Eli Branson, and Alexander MacLean, in A.O. 12:35, 100; A.O. 13:79, 117, 122, 138.

[25]Claims of Captain Kenneth Stewart, Lieutenant Kenneth Stewart, Neil Colbreath, Neil McArthur, John Legett, Alexander McRae, and Thomas Wier, in A.O. 13:118, 121, 124, 138.

[26]*SRNC,* XXIII: 985.

[27]*SRNC,* XXIV: 11.

[28]Deposition of George Redman, July 27, 1778, Rowan County Civil and Criminal Cases, N.C.A., hereinafter cited as Rowan Cases.

[29]Order against James Glen, March 22, 1778, Rowan Cases; Examination of James Glen, March 27, 1778, Rowan Cases.

[30]Claim of Neil Snodgrass, A.O. 13:123; Claims of William McQueen, Jane Stenhouse, Archibald Hamilton, in A.O. 12:100; A.O. 13:138; Collin Shaw to Mrs. Shaw, October 18, 1777, Shaw Papers, N.C.A.

[31]Deposition of Thomas Lester, September 4, 1777, Chowan County Papers, N.C.A.; Deposition of Daniel Fulford, August 26, 1777, Chowan County Papers, N.C.A.; *CRNC,* IX:638; *SRNC,* XXIII: 960.

[32]Deposition of Benjamin Morris, August 2, 1777, Bertie County Criminal Papers, N.C.A.

[33]Unless otherwise indicated, information about the Llewelyn conspiracy is based on Edenton District Superior Court Records, 1777; Prosecution Docket, Edenton District Superior Court, 1778; Edenton District Court Papers, 1777; Chowan County Papers, 1777, all in N.C.A. Many of the depositions in Edenton District Superior Court Records have been printed in "Affidavits relating to loyalists and tories during the Revolution," *The North Carolina Historical and Genealogical Register,* II (1901), 208-217, 390-405, 569-577.

[34]Deposition of Salvinas Buttrey, Edenton District Superior Court Records, 1777, N.C.A.

[35]Deposition of John Stewart, Edenton District Superior Court Records, 1777.

[36]Martin County Tax Lists, 1779, N.C.A.; Bertie County Tax Lists, 1781, N.C.A.; Martin County 1787 Census, N.C.A. The 1790 census indicates that at that time approximately one-fourth of the group were slaveowners. *SRNC,* XXVI, *passim.*

[37]Depositions of David and Joseph Taylor, June 4, 1777, Edenton District Superior Court Records, N.C.A.

[38]Militia and Continental Returns, 1779-1780, Troop Returns, box 3, Military Collection, N.C.A.; Bertie County Revolutionary War Papers, N.C.A.

[39]Jones to Burke, August 6, 1777, Thomas Burke Papers, N.C.A.

[40]*SRNC,* XI: 776-777; XII: 115-116, 118-119, 122, 268-272, 274, 277-278; XXII: 929.

[41]Beasley to Caswell, December 2, 1777, *SRNC,* XI: 816.

[42]For this information I am grateful to Jeffrey Crow, who is preparing a study of the Llewelyn conspiracy.

[43]Examination of Henrey Daniel, August 14, 1778, Rowan Cases. One wants to think that this fierce soul was not the Henry O'Daniel who in 1781 joined Cornwallis at Hillsborough for three weeks, returned home to Orange County and surrendered to a justice of the peace, and was

pardoned by Governor Thomas Burke on condition that he immediately join General John Butler's militia. *SRNC,* XXII: 576; Henry O'Daniel recognizance, June 10, 1781, Hillsborough District Criminal Action Papers, 1782, N.C.A.

[44]David Fanning, for example, served in the South Carolina Militia for more than a year. Claim of David Fanning, A.O. 13:138; Ontario Bureau of Archives, *Second Report,* compiled by Alexander Fraser (Toronto: L.K. Cameron, 1905), 241.

[45]The examining justice of the peace marked through the qualifying words which follow "&c." Examination of Michael Miller *et al.,* January 19, 1779, Salisbury District Court Records, N.C.A.; Rowan Committee of Safety, *passim;* Salisbury District Trial and Minute Docket, March 4, 1777, N.C.A.

[46]March, 1779, recognizances, Salisbury District State Docket, N.C.A.

[47]Deposition of James Dickey, March 12, 1778, Rowan Cases.

[48]Deposition of John Haggen, July 27, 1778, Rowan Cases.

[49]Deposition of William Cathey, July 10, 1778, Rowan Cases.

[50]Deposition of Joseph Cronkleton, n.d. [after June, 1778], Rowan Cases.

[51]Deposition of Thomas Jenings, May 16, 1778, Rowan Cases.

[52]*SRNC,* XIV: 261; Petition of Charles McLean, n.d. [filed August-September, 1780], Legislative Papers, N.C.A.

[53]John Hamilton statement in claim of Neil Colbreath, A.O. 13:118.

[54]Claims of Archibald McDougald, Daniel McNeill, John Hamilton, Neil McArthur in A.O. 12:100; A.O. 13:25, 121, 138; Neil McArthur receipt, British Headquarters Papers, No. 4211, P.A.C., hereinafter cited as B.H.P.

[55]In 1780, 104 of the 125 persons listed for McCrainie District were penalized, but only two of them for refusing the oath. Cumberland County List of Taxables, 1778, 1779, 1780, N.C.A.

[56]Minutes of the Tryon County Committee of Safety, Secretary of State's Papers, N.C.A.; Claim of Jonas Bedford, A.O. 13:108.

[57]Ferguson to Cornwallis, June 22, 1780, Cornwallis Papers, P.R.O.

[58]Clinton Proclamation, June 3, 1780, C.O. 5: 264; Edward McCrady, *South Carolina in the Revolution, 1775-1780* (New York: Macmillan, 1901), 554.

[59]David Schenck, *North Carolina, 1780-'81. Being a History of the Invasion of the Carolinas by the British Army under Lord Cornwallis* (Raleigh: Edwards and Broughton, 1889), 52, quotes Joseph Graham's Narrative.

[60]Cornwallis reprimanded Moore for raising the men before the appointed time. When Cornwallis camped near Ramsour's Mill the following January, the men who had joined Moore did not greet him. Claim of Nicholas Welch, A.O. 13:124; Smith, *Loyalists and Redcoats,* 142.

[61]Claims of Andrew Hamm, David Harkey, and Samuel Bryan, in A.O. 13:117, 138; Banastre Tarleton, *A History of the Campaigns of 1780 and 1781, in the Southern Provinces of North America* (London: T. Cadell, 1787), 91.

[62]Hamm was captured at Yorktown and settled in New Brunswick after the war. Claim of Andrew Hamm, A.O. 12:35, 65; Rowan County Deed Books, Office of the Register of Deeds, Rowan County Courthouse, Deed Books, V: 34, 35; VII: 277, 278, microfilm copies in N.C.A., hereinafter cited as Rowan Deed Books; Jethro Rumple, *A History of Rowan County, North Carolina.* Bicentennial Edition. (Baltimore: Regional Publishing Company, 1974; original published Salisbury, 1881), 136-137.

[63]The Blewers were in Nova Scotia and New Brunswick for a few years after the war, but by 1790 they were living in South Carolina. Claims of Jacob, Peter, and John Blewer, A.O. 13: 35; Mecklenburg County Court Minutes, April, 1778, N.C.A.; Bureau of the Census, *Heads of Families at the First Census of the United States Taken in the Year 1790: South Carolina* (Washington: Government Printing Office, 1908), 36, 97; Mecklenburg County Deed Books, Office of the Register of Deeds, Mecklenburg County Courthouse, Deed Books, VII: 279; XIII: 878, 913, microfilm copies in N.C.A., hereinafter cited as Mecklenburg Deed Books.

[64]Cornwallis to Sir Henry Clinton, April 10, 1781, *SRNC,* XVII: 1011.

[65]Alexander Martin to ________, November 17, 1781, Miscellaneous Papers, N.C.A. indicates that contemporaries regarded McNeill and not Fanning as the leader of the attack.

[66]Robert Gray, "Colonel Robert Gray's Observations on the War in Carolina," *South Carolina Historical and Genealogical Magazine,* XI, 145, 140-159.

[67]*SRNC,* XIV: 744-745; Davie to Jethro Sumner, October 6, 1780, William R. Davie Papers, S.H.C.

[68]John Penn to Thomas Taylor, September 21, 1780, Board of War, Revolutionary War, Military Collection, N.C.A., hereinafter cited as Board of War.

[69][Alexander Martin] to John Butler, November 25, 1780, Board of War.

[70]Deposition of Randal Southerlin, n.d. [marked "1781"], Chowan County Papers, N.C.A.

[71]Deposition of William Nichols, June 28, 1781, Legislative Papers, N.C.A.

[72]Proclamation of Alexander Martin, November 25, 1780, Board of War.

[73]Petition of John Evans, n.d. [filed August-September, 1780] Legislative Papers, N.C.A.; Reprieve order for Meredith Edwards *et al.,* n.d., [1781-82], Thomas Burke Papers, S.H.C.; Craven County Court Minutes, September, 1780, September, 1782, N.C.A.; Commons Resolution, May 8, 1777, Legislative Papers, N.C.A.; *SRNC,* XXIV: 157-158, 268.

[74]George W. Troxler, "Pyle's Massacre, February 23, 1781," (Burlington: Alamance County Historical Association, 1973).

[75]All were found guilty and were fined a total of £1,540 specie as damages. Chatham County Court Minutes, May, 1782, N.C.A.

[76]Muster rolls of North Carolina militia, Treasury Papers, 50: 5, P.R.O.; Muster rolls of South Carolina Light Dragoons, British Military Records, "C." P.A.C.; Muster rolls of North Carolina Volunteers, Lawrence Collection, Chipman Papers, P.A.C.

[77]*SRNC,* XVI: 244; XXVI: *passim;* Chatham County Court Minutes, August and November, 1782, N.C.A.; Will of John Pyle, Chatham County Will Books A: 25; Chatham County Deed Books, Office of the Register of Deeds, Chatham County Courthouse, Deed Books, M: 634, C-N, T,V, *passim,* microfilm copies in N.C.A., hereinafter cited as Chatham Deed Books.

[78]*CRNC,* X: 545-546; *SRNC,* XII: 252; XXIV: 11-12, 209-210, 263-268, 348-353, 376-377, 424-429. For a description of the laws, see Robert O. DeMond, *The Loyalists in North Carolina during the Revolution* (Durham: Duke University Press, 1940), 153-169.

[79]*SRNC,* XXIV: 490.

[80]Governor Alexander Martin demanded that the judges explain to the legislature why they had disregarded Mallet's exemption in the act. Martin to Samuel Ashe, Samuel Spencer, and John Williams, October 10, 1783, *SRNC,* XVI: 879; Wilmington District Superior Court Minutes, 1782, 1783, November, 1785, June, 1786, N.C.A. It is a truism that England's law is one of her most lasting gifts to the former colonies. At the time of these loyalist cases, the state's attorney appealed to a fourteenth-century English statute regarding pardons, and the court was still using stationery bearing the royal watermark.

[81]William Campbell to Frederick Gregg, December 25, 1787, Claim of Frederick Gregg, A.O. 13:119.

[82]Mecklenburg Deed Books, XIII: 878, 913. The British government had compensated Blewer for the loss of the land. Claim of Peter Blewer A.O. 12:68.

[83]List of goods attached from James Hamilton, December 14, 1781, Rowan Cases; List of James Hamilton's confiscated property, n.d. [filed 1782], Rowan Cases; Claim of James Hamilton, A.O. 13:119; Hillsborough District Court Records, January, 1782.

[84]Claim of Connor Dowd, A.O. 12:99, 13:118; *SRNC,* XIV: 856; Chatham Deed Books, B: 25; 132, 299. One of Dowd's mills was where the Carolina Power and Light Company dam at Carbonton is now. Blackwell P. Robinson, *A History of Moore County, North Carolina, 1747-1847* (Southern Pines: Moore County Historical Association, 1956), 41-42, 64-65.

[85]*CRNC,* X: 839, 559, 602-603; Claim of Connor Dowd, A.O. 13:118.

[86]Eventually the claims commissioners in London allowed him £567 of the £5,524 he claimed.

Claim of Connor Dowd, A.O. 13:118; Cumberland County Miscellaneous Papers, July, 1779, N.C.A.; Cumberland County List of Taxables, 1777, 1779, N.C.A.; *SRNC,* XI: 626-631.

[87]Chatham County Court Minutes, November, 1782, N.C.A.

[88]*SRNC,* XIX: 548, 551, 639, 644, 696; XXIV: 638-639.

[89]Norman Morison to Alexander Morison, February 28, 1784, claim of Alexander Morison, A.O. 13:122.

[90]Chatham Deed Books, C: 382, 531, 532; F: 243. Dowd's presence is attested by his serving as a security for his mother following her charge with a misdeameanor in 1783. Chatham County Court Minutes, November, 1783, N.C.A.

[91]Chatham Deed Books, C: 176, 227, 458, 535, 548, 581.

[92]Alexander Morison to Dowd, December 18, 1786, claim of Connor Dowd, A.O. 13:118.

[93]Mary Dowd to Dowd, January 9, 1789, claim of Connor Dowd, A.O. 13:118.

[94]*SRNC,* XXVI: 780; Chatham Deed Books, E: 111-112; H: 243.

[95]*SRNC,* XXI: 278, 342, 399, 710; XXV: 46.

[96]Chatham Deed Books, E: 215, 217, G: 32, 71; H: 95, 310; J: 443; K: 55, 126, 199, 221.

[97]Chatham Deed Books, M: 122; Chatham County Court Minutes, November, 1790, May, 1792; Deposition of John Beck, October 31, 1788, Chatham County Miscellaneous Papers; Rosannah Dowd folder, Chatham County Guardians' Accounts; Wilmington District Superior Court, June, 1788; Fayetteville District Equity Minute Docket, November 2, 1792, April 3, 1783, October 23, 1794; *Fayetteville Gazette,* November 27, 1792, all in N.C.A. Connor Dowd warrant to survey, April 27, 1780, Chatham County, Land Grant Records of North Carolina, Office of the Secretary of State, Raleigh, lists John Beck as a chain bearer.

[98]Deed to Aaron Tyson and Company, Chatham Deed Books, N: 190; Chatham County Court Minutes, August, 1791; Will of Judith Dowd, Chatham County Will Books, A: 88; Judith Dowd inventory, Chatham County Estates Papers, all in N.C.A.

[99]Marmaduke Jones to Frederick Gregg, July 8, 1784, claim of Frederick Gregg, A.O. 13:119.

[100]In 1811 he returned again, in an unsuccessful attempt to take possession of land in Chatham and Cumberland counties which his father had willed to him. Instead, he took some of his father's slaves to Nova Scotia, where they escaped, and where he died in 1818. A.W. Savary, (ed.), *Col. David Fanning's Narrative of his Exploits and Adventures as a Loyalist of North Carolina in the American Revolution* (Toronto: 1908), 55; Claim of Daniel McNeill A.O. 12:35, 65; A.O. 13:91, 138; Wilmington District Miscellaneous Court Records, December, 1785.

[101]Alexander McAuslin Estate Papers, Chatham County Estates, N.C.A.; Petition of Alexander McAuslan, 1787, Unused Petitions, P.A.N.S.; Claim of Alexander McAuslan, A.O. 12:37, 13:80.

[102]Maclellan to Gernon, May 15, 1786, claim of James Gernon, A.O. 12:35.

[103]Claim of heirs of Matthew Colvill, A.O. 12:37.

[104]Claims of Normand McLeod and Duncan McNabb, A.O. 13:121.

[105]Muster rolls of North Carolina Highlanders, North Carolina Volunteers, and Royal North Carolina Regiment, Lawrence Collection, Chipman Papers, P.A.C.

[106]Treasury Papers 50:4, p. 173; and 50:5, pp. 2, 7, P.R.O., microfilm copies in North Carolina Collection, University of North Carolina, Chapel Hill; Claim of McDougald, A.O. 13:25; Claim of Kenneth Stewart, A.O. 12:36.

[107]Treasurer's and Comptroller's Papers, boxes 1 and 4, N.C.A.; Anson County Deed Books, Office of the Register of Deeds, Anson County Courthouse, Deed Books, N and O: 84, microfilm copies in N.C.A.; Bahamas Register General, B/1, 157, 159, microfilm copies in P.K. Yonge Library of Florida History, University of Florida, Gainesville; Petition of Samuel Williams, [1794], Upper Canada Land Petitions, P.A.C.; Claims of Jacob and Samuel Williams, A.O. 12:36, 65, 109; A.O. 13:82, 138.

[108]Claim of Jacob Williams, A.O. 12:36.

[109]Claim of Ann McLeod, A.O. 12:100; A.O. 13:121; Claim of Donald Morrison, A.O. 12:100;

Claim of Alexander Telfair, A.O. 12:102, A.O. 13:123, 124.

[110]Claim of Jane Stenhouse, A.O. 13:137; Claim of Mary Gray, A.O. 13:118; Claim of John Thompson, A.O. 12:102; Claim of Joseph Rathell, A.O. 13:123.

[111]B.H.P., Nos. 6159, 6475, 7468; C.O. 5:560, 482-484, 493-498, 805-820.

[112]C.O. 5:560, 848-850.

[113]Claim of John Hamilton, A.O. 13:95.

[114]Claim of James Cruden, A.O. 12:37; *East Florida Gazette,* May 3, 1783; Wilbur Henry Siebert, *Loyalists in East Florida, 1774-1785* (Deland, Florida: The Florida State Historical Society, 1929) I, 124.

[115]Joseph Bryne Lockey, *East Florida 1783-1785: A File of Documents Assembled and Many of them Translated,* ed. John Walton Caughey (Berkley: University of California Press, 1949), 195-196, 288-292, hereinafter cited as Lockey, *East Florida;* Charles Loch Mowat, *East Florida as a British Province, 1763-1784* (Berkeley: University of California Press, 1943), 243; *The Morning Chronicle and London Advertiser,* September 1, 1784, p. 2.

[116]Lockey, *East Florida,* 221.

[117]Lockey, *East Florida,* 302, 312-314, 484.

[118]*CRNC,* IX: 1153; X: 437; *SRNC,* XI: 715; XV: 82; XVI: 972-973, 995; XVII: 156-157; XVIII: 806, 809.

[119]Unless otherwise indicated, the following account is based on Thelma Peters, "Loyalists and the Plantation Period in the Bahamas," (Unpublished Ph.D. dissertation, University of Florida, 1960).

[120]*CRNC,* X: 72-73, 141, 173, 175, 586, 827, 846; *SRNC,* XI: 392; Bahamas Register General, A/1, p. 177; *Bahama Gazette* (Nassau), January 7, 1791.

[121]In 1790 Hamilton was appointed British Consul to Norfolk, Virginia. Memorial of Southern Loyalists to Lord Sydney, Foreign Office Papers 4:1, P.R.O., transcript in English Records, N.C.A.; Lorenzo Sabine, *Biographical Sketches of Loyalists of the American Revolution with an Historical Essay* (Port Washington, New York: Reprint by Kennikat Press, 1966), I, 512; Bahamas Register General, B/1, p. 26, A/1, p. 20.

[122]Barbara Gorely Teller, "The Case of Some Inhabitants of East Florida, 1767-1785," *Florida Historical Quarterly* XXXIII (1954), 106.

[123]Carole Watterson Troxler, "The Migration of Carolina and Georgia Loyalists to Nova Scotia and New Brunswick," (Unpublished Ph.D. dissertation, University of North Carolina at Chapel Hill, 1974). Complete documentation for the following account is contained therein.

[124]Warrants to survey for the King's Carolina Rangers, the South Carolina Regiment [*sic*], and the Royal North Carolina Regiment, 1784, P.A.N.S.; Lawrence Collection, Chipman Papers, Vol. 24, pp. 253-261, P.A.C.

[125]Lawrence Collection, Chipman Papers, Vol. 24, p. 325, P.A.C.

[126]McInnes stuck it out. He was instrumental in getting a road from the area to Halifax and became a justice of the peace. He died there by 1818. P.A.N.S., Manuscript Vol. 214, 80, 129; Treasury Papers 50: 8-28, 31-48, transcripts of North Carolina material in English Records, N.C.A.; Claim of Miles McInnes, A.O. 12:100, A.O. 13:121.

[127]Governor John Parr to Lord Shelburne, May 1, 1785, Shelburne Papers, Vol. 88, p. 81, transcripts in P.A.C.

[128]James W. St.G. Walker, "The Black Loyalists in Nova Scotia and Sierra Leone," (Unpublished Ph.D. dissertation, Dalhousie University, 1973), 9, hereinafter cited as Walker, "Black Loyalists."

[129]*Saint John Gazette,* June 29, 1792.

[130]Royal North Carolina Regiment warrant to survey, February 1, 1785, P.A.N.S.; Lawrence Collection, Chipman Papers, Vol. 24, 256-259, P.A.C.; Shelburne, Nova Scotia, Special Sessions, August 5, 1786, P.A.C.

[131]See Walker, "Black Loyalists," 27-158, for the causes and nature of the black loyalist identity.

[132]"Petition of the Free Negroes now living at Manchester," Unused Petitions, 1786-1787, P.A.N.S.; Petition of Chedabucto Blacks, [1788], Unused Petitions, P.A.N.S.

[133]Walker, "Black Loyalists," 159-192.

[134]Petition of Thomas Peters to William Syndham Grenville, n.d., enclosed to Henry Dundas to Parr, August 6, 1791, C.O. 217:63, pp. 58-59; "Enquiry into the Complaint of Thomas Peters," enclosed in Richard Bulkeley to Dundas, March 19, 1792, C.O. 217:63, pp. 165-176.

[135]Statement of the Sierra Leone Company, enclosed in Dundas to Parr, August 6, 1791, C.O. 217:63, pp. 60-61.

[136][Dundas] to Parr, August 6, 1791, C.O. 217:72, pp. 79-81.

[137]John Clarkson to Henry Thornton, December 1, 1791, Clarkson's Mission to America, P.A.N.S.; Hartshorne to Thornton, February 9, 1792, C.O. 217:63, pp. 373-375; Bulkeley to Dundas, November 29, 1791, C.O. 217:63, p. 144; G. Haliburton, "The Nova Scotia Settlers of 1792," *Sierra Leone Studies,* new series, IX (1957), 18-19; Anthoney Kirk-Greene, "David George: The Nova Scotia Experience," *Sierra Leone Studies,* new series, XIV (1960), 108.

[138]"List of the blacks in Birch Town who gave in their Names for Sierra Leone in November, 1791," C.O. 217: 63, pp. 362-366.

[139]"David George," *The Baptist Annual Register,* I, 482.

[140]Bulkeley to Dundas, February 3, 1792, C.O. 217:63, p. 153.

[141]Stephen Skinner to Dundas, n.d., C.O. 217:63, pp. 357-360.

[142]Walker, "Black Loyalists," 250-258.

[143]Walker, "Black Loyalists," 259-263.

[144]See Robert W. July, *The Origins of Modern African Thought: Its Development in West Africa during the nineteenth and twentieth centuries* (New York: Frederick A. Praeger, 1967), 56-65.

[145]Ernest Alexander Cruikshank, (ed.), *The Correspondence of Governor John Graves Simcoe, with Allied Documents, Relating to His Administration of the Government of Upper Canada, 1789-1796* (Toronto: Ontario Historical Society, 1923-1931), IV, 313, 317, hereinafter cited as Simcoe Papers.

[146]Simcoe Papers, III, 56; Upper Canada Land Petitions, 1792-1805, *passim,* P.A.C.

[147]Samuel Patrick had served in the North Carolina Volunteers and had accompanied the British to Charles Town on the evacuation of Wilmington. Lawrence Collection, Chipman Papers, Vol. 27, pp. 346-347, P.A.C.

[148]Petition of James Ozburn, 1798, Upper Canada Land Petitions, P.A.C.; Upper Canada Land Book B published in Department of Public Records and Archives of Ontario, *Nineteenth Report* (Toronto: Herbert H. Ball, 1931), 86-87; Rowan Deed Books, IV: 329, 336, 375; VII: 100, 354, 355, 356, VIII: 79, 105; Rowan County Tax Lists, Davis District, 1778, 1784, 1785, manuscript and microfilm copies, N.C.A.; Rowan Committee of Safety; Salisbury District Superior Court Minutes, March, 1783, and September, 1785, N.C.A.; Rowan County Court of Pleas and Quarter Session Minutes, November 6, 1782, N.C.A.; *CRNC,* VI: 1077; VIII: 64, 856; X: 441, 433-444; *SRNC,* XVII: 315; XX: 59, 496; XXI: 72, 1039; XXVI: 1028; James S. Brawley, *The Rowan Story, 1753-1953* (Salisbury: Rowan Printing Company, 1953), 351-357. The pioneer student of southern loyalists inferred that the Major Spurgeon or Spurgin killed at Beech Island, South Carolina, in March, 1779, was William Spurgin of Rowan County. Siebert, *Loyalists in East Florida,* II, 69.

[149]Petition of Reubin Garlick *et al.,* 1786, Lower Canada Land Papers, P.A.C.; Rowan County Tax Lists, 1778, N.C.A.; Rowan Cases, 1784; Rowan Deed Books, XIV: 640; *SRNC,* XXVI: 1044; Second Census of the United States, 1800: Rowan County, North Carolina, population schedule, microfilm of National Archives manuscript copy, N.C.A.; Petition of Albright Spring, 1801, Upper Canada Land Petition of Albright Spring, 1801, Upper Canada Land Petitions, P.A.C.

NOTE ON SOURCES

The most directly useful sources for studying North Carolina loyalists are the claims that 226 of them made to the British government in pursuit of compensation for their losses as loyalists: Audit Office Papers, 1765-1790, American Loyalist Claims, P.R.O. Transcripts of the North Carolina claims are among the English Records Collection in N.C.A. This should be supplemented by notes made by the claims commissioners, published as Ontario Bureau of Archives, *Second Report*, compiled by Alexander Fraser (Toronto: L.K. Cameron, 1905). The claims provide a wealth of detail not found elsewhere. Care must be maintained in the use of them, however, for the claimants were tempted to exaggerate both the value of their property and the extent of their services to the British. The student must be, as the British government's claims commissioners were, ever alert to fraud. Moreover, it should not be assumed that the statements made in the claims apply as well to North Carolina loyalists who did not make claims. The North Carolina claimants' statements about their national origins, occupations, amount of claims, services to the British forces, and geographic distribution are conveniently analyzed in Wallace Brown, *The King's Friends: The Composition and Motives of the American Loyalist Claimants* (Providence: Brown University Press, 1965), 333-336. A useful critique of this and other uses of loyalists' claims is Eugene R. Fingerhut, "Uses and Abuses of the American Loyalists' Claims: A Critique of Quantitative Analysis," *William and Mary Quarterly,* Third Series, XXV (1968), 245-258.

The myriad of county records in the N.C.A. are essential. Their use is best approached through the district and county court records. Especially useful are the extant criminal action papers. The availability and completeness of tax records vary among the counties; land records are a helpful supplement.

The Treasurer's and Comptroller's Papers contain records of the commissioners of confiscated loyalists' estates. Other state manuscript records in which loyalists are prominent include Legislative Papers, Governors' Papers, Secretary of State's Papers, and Military Collection, Revolutionary War. Of the many private manuscript collections in N.C.A. which contain loyalist material, the richest seem to be the Archibald Maclaine Papers, the Shaw Papers, and the Thomas Burke Papers.

The loyalist experience in many of the areas to which North Carolinians emigrated are treated in the following: Esther Clark Wright, *The Loyalists of New Brunswick* (Moncton, New Brunswick: privately printed, 1955); Neil McKinnon, "Nova Scotia: The Loyalist Period," (Unpublished Ph. D. dissertation, Queen's University, 1969); Gerald M. Craig, *Upper Canada: The Formative Years, 1784-1841* (Toronto: McClelland and Stewart Limited, 1963); Thelma Peters, "Loyalists and the Plantation Period in the Bahamas," (Unpublished Ph. D. dissertation, University of Florida, 1960); Mary Beth Norton, *The British-Americans: The Loyalist Exiles in England, 1774-1789* (Boston: Little, Brown, and Company, 1972); Charles Loch Mowat, *East Florida as a British Province, 1763-1784* (Berkeley and Los Angeles: University of California Press, 1943); Wilbur Henry Siebert, *The Legacy of the American Revolution to the British West Indies and Bahamas; a chapter out of the history of the American Loyalists* (Columbus: Ohio State University Press, 1913); Wilbur Henry Siebert, "The Loyalists in West Florida and the Natchez District," *Mississippi Valley Historical Review*, II (1915-16), 465-483. Siebert's introductory notes in *The Journal of Alexander Chesney, A South Carolina Loyalist in the Revolution and After* (Columbus: Ohio State University Press, 1921) are useful. His *Loyalists in East Florida, 1774-1785* (Deland, Florida: The Florida State Historical Society, 1929) includes compensation claims for losses incurred by the cession of East Florida. Some North Carolina loyalists are among the claimants. Other documents for the loyalist experience in East Florida are in Joseph Byrne Lockey, *East Florida, 1783-1785: A File of Documents Assembled, and Many of them Translated* (Berkeley and Los Angeles: University of California Press, 1949). The Lockey Collection from which they are drawn and other manuscript sources for the East Florida loyalist experience are in the P.K. Yonge Library of Florida History, University of Florida, Gainesville, Florida.

Also at the P.K. Yonge Library of Florida History are microfilm copies of the records of the Bahamas Register General, Nassau. This and the *Bahama Gazette* (Nassau, 1784-1800) are basic for the study of North Carolina loyalists in the Bahamas. Also of interest is a manuscript by Lydia Austin Parrish, "Records of some Southern Loyalists, Being a Collection of Manuscripts about some eighty families, most of whom immigrated to the Bahamas during and after the American Revolution," in the Widener Library, Harvard University. Microfilm copies are available in the P.K. Yonge Library of Florida History and the Georgia Department of Archives and History, Atlanta.

Land records are a useful approach to North Carolina loyalists in Nova Scotia and New Brunswick. A convenient and reliable abstract of New

Brunswick land records is New Brunswick Land Grants and Petitions, 1784-1860 in P.A.C. Nova Scotia land grants, warrants to survey, and escheats have been compiled by Marion Gilroy in *Loyalists and Land Settlement in Nova Scotia* (Halifax: Public Archives of Nova Scotia, 1937). Further records are available in the Public Archives of Nova Scotia and the Public Archives of New Brunswick. W.O. Raymone, (ed.), *The Winslowd Papers* (Saint John: New Brunswick Historical Society, 1901) is of interest. Ward Chipman was Muster-Master of Provincial Forces during the war and a lawyer in New Brunswick afterwards. His records and letters contain some material about North Carolinians. They are the Ward Chipman Papers, New Brunswick Museum, and the Ward Chipman Papers, Lawrence Collection, P.A.C. Some Nova Scotia and New Brunswick material of North Carolina interest is contained in James Hannay, "New Brunswick, Report on Burying Grounds," 1908; Charles Inglis Papers [bishop of Nova Scotia], Amos Botsford Papers [Loyalists' provisions agent], and transcripts of the Shelburne Papers and the Chatham Papers, all in P.A.C. Microfilm copies of P.A.C.'s British Headquarters Papers [Sir Guy Carleton Papers] are in S.C.A. Some of John Clarkson's material has been published as Charles Bruce Fergusson (ed.), *Clarkson's Mission to America, 1791-1792* (Halifax: Public Archives of Nova Scotia, 1971). Information about individual blacks in Nova Scotia, including birthplaces, appears in "Muster-Book of Free Black Settlement of Birchtown, 1784," Shelburne, Nova Scotia, in P.A.C. and in "Lists of the blacks in Birch Town who gave in their Names for Sierra Leone in November 1791," C.O. 217:63, pp. 362-366. Memoirs of black loyalists are Boston King, "Memoirs of the Life of Boston King, a Black Preacher, Written by Himself, During his Residence at Kingswood-School," *Arminian Magazine,* XXI (1798), 105-111, 157-161, 209-265, and [David George], "David George," *The Baptist Annual Register,* I, 473-483. Most of George's narrative also appears in David Benedict, *A General History of the Baptist Denomination in America, and other Parts of the World* (Boston: Manning and Loring, 1813), I, 288-295.

Materials for North Carolina loyalists in Upper Canada are scattered in the Haldimand Papers (transcripts in P.A.C.), in Ernest Alexander Cruikshank (ed.), *The Correspondence of Governor John Graves Simcoe, with Allied Documents Relating to His Administration of the Government of Upper Canada, 1789-1796* (Toronto: Ontario Historical Society, 4 volumes, 1923-1931), and in Upper Canada Land Petitions, P.A.C. Upper Canada Land Books A-D, useful for the loyalist period, are published in Department of Public Records and Archives of Ontario, *Seventeenth Report, Eighteenth Report, Nineteenth Report, Twentieth Report* (Toronto: Herbert H. Ball, 1929-1932, respectively) and are a convenient starting point.

About the Author

Born in LaGrange, Georgia, Carole Watterson Troxler earned an A.B. at the University of Georgia before receiving her M.A. and Ph.D. from the University of North Carolina at Chapel Hill, where she was a Woodrow Wilson Fellow. A member of Phi Beta Kappa, she is currently an Assistant Professor of History at Elon College. Married to George W. Troxler, who is also a member of the faculty at Elon College, she is involved in the Program for Loyalist Studies and Publications and holds memberships in the American Historical Association, the Conference on British Studies, and the Southern Historical Association.

3 4200 00010 55

N.C.
975.603
T
C3
Troxler, Carole Watterson
The loyalist experience in North Carolina
DISCARDED
from
New Hanover County Public Library
NEW HANOVER COUNTY PUBLIC LIBRARY
WILMINGTON, NORTH CAROLINA